What Are the Dangers of Online Scams?

Other titles in the *Issues Today* series include:

How Can Gun Violence Be Stopped?
How Does Fake News Threaten Society?
How Should America Deal with Undocumented Immigrants?
How Should Extremist Content Be Regulated on Social Media?
How Should Society Respond to the Refugee Crisis?
How Has the #MeToo Movement Changed Society?

ISSUES TODAY

What Are the Dangers of Online Scams?

John Allen

San Diego, CA

© 2021 ReferencePoint Press, Inc.
Printed in the United States

For more information, contact:
ReferencePoint Press, Inc.
PO Box 27779
San Diego, CA 92198
www.ReferencePointPress.com

ALL RIGHTS RESERVED.
No part of this work covered by the copyright hereon may be reproduced or used in any form or by any means—graphic, electronic, or mechanical, including photocopying, recording, taping, web distribution, or information storage retrieval systems—without the written permission of the publisher.

LIBRARY OF CONGRESS CATALOGING-IN-PUBLICATION DATA

Names: Allen, John, 1957- author.
Title: What are the dangers of online scams? / by John Allen.
Description: San Diego, CA : ReferencePoint Press, [2021] | Series: Issues today | Includes bibliographical references and index.
Identifiers: LCCN 2020012333 (print) | LCCN 2020012334 (ebook) | ISBN 9781682828878 (library binding) | ISBN 9781682828885 (ebook)
Subjects: LCSH: Internet fraud--Juvenile literature. | Computer crimes--Juvenile literature.
Classification: LCC HV6773.15.C56 A45 2021 (print) | LCC HV6773.15.C56 (ebook) | DDC 364.16/3--dc23
LC record available at https://lccn.loc.gov/2020012333
LC ebook record available at https://lccn.loc.gov/2020012334

CONTENTS

Introduction   **6**
A Scam on Online Gamers

Chapter One   **10**
The Growing Problem of Online Scams

Chapter Two   **22**
How Victims Are Harmed by Online Scams

Chapter Three   **33**
Why People Fall for Online Scams

Chapter Four   **44**
Can Online Scams Be Stopped?

Chapter Five   **56**
Avoiding Online Scams

Source Notes   67
Organizations and Websites   72
For Further Research   74
Index   75
Picture Credits   79
About the Author   80

INTRODUCTION

A Scam on Online Gamers

Online gamers consider themselves among the most tech-savvy people in the world. Yet many of them have been snared by a game-related online scam. The scam involves the wildly popular online game *Fortnite*. Since its introduction in 2017, *Fortnite* has attracted hundreds of millions of players around the world. They try to survive in the game's digital world by collecting tools and weapons, building fortresses, and defeating other players in battle. Although free to play, *Fortnite* makes most of its revenue—$2.4 billion in 2018—by getting players to pay real money for in-game currency, called V-Bucks. The V-Bucks can be used to buy special characters and so-called emotes for dancing and taunting other players on the battlefield. But thousands of scam sites have sprung up to cash in on the game's popularity.

In an October 2018 study, the online security company ZeroFOX announced it had found more than forty-seven hundred bogus *Fortnite* websites. Hackers design the sites to mimic the colorful look of the genuine *Fortnite* game. The sites sell fake V-Bucks or offer V-Bucks in exchange for personal information, including credit card numbers. The scammers have also used social media, YouTube videos, and fake apps to deceive unwary gamers. Despite warnings, thousands of players have been fooled by the scammers, leading to sizable losses from fraudulent sales and identity theft. "Young users are more vulnerable. They may not be as aware that it is a scam," says Nevada's Senior Deputy Attorney General Laura Tucker. "Kids want to get more V-Bucks so they can purchase characters and dances and things like that. So, the scam is basically exploiting that [urge]."[1]

A Growing Risk for Internet Users

As more people conduct business and social activity on the internet, the opportunities for online scams have exploded. The costs to businesses and individuals have likewise skyrocketed. A study from the Center for Strategic and International Studies and the computer security firm McAfee estimates the total annual cost of cybercrime to the global economy at $600 billion. The cybersecurity company SEON estimates that every dollar lost to online frauds and scams ends up costing businesses up to three dollars in indirect charges. Online scams also

> "Kids want to get more V-Bucks so they can purchase characters and dances and things like that. So, the scam is basically exploiting that [urge]."[1]
>
> —Laura Tucker, senior deputy attorney general in Nevada

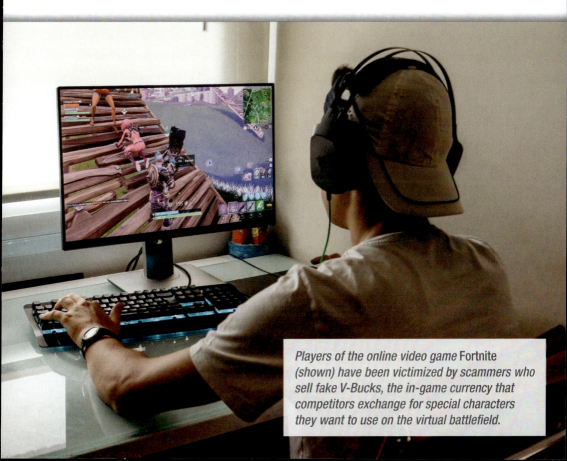

Players of the online video game *Fortnite* (shown) have been victimized by scammers who sell fake V-Bucks, the in-game currency that competitors exchange for special characters they want to use on the virtual battlefield.

expose individuals to losses of time and money. Unsuspecting users on the internet can lose a few hundred dollars on a bogus shopping site or much larger sums by giving up a bank account number.

Online scams take many different forms. There are phishing schemes via email or text message, fake websites and pop-up windows, and deceptive fund-raising ploys. A seemingly routine request to change or verify a password can enable hackers to infiltrate a network. The Anti-Phishing Working Group notes that the number of phishing attempts reported each month worldwide approaches one hundred thousand. Users can even be swindled by fake security companies that promise to protect them from scams and instead plant malware on their computers. Online scams target users of all ages, including—as in the *Fortnite* scams—supposedly tech-savvy young people. However, elderly users are considered to be especially vulnerable. "Older adults make great targets because they have accumulated assets over time and are living off their savings," says Larry Santucci, coauthor of a report about elderly financial victims for the Federal Reserve Bank of Philadelphia. "Some are also very lonely or socially isolated, which makes them susceptible to exploitation."[2]

Each time a person shops online or surfs the internet, he or she runs the risk of being scammed. With oceans of personal and financial data stored online, even people without computers can suffer from cyberattacks on their credit card company or doctor's office. In 2019 hackers invaded the data banks at Capital One Financial Corporation, gaining access to the personal records of more than 100 million customers.

Preying on Users' Emotions

Online scammers prey on users' emotions, such as fear, greed, sympathy, and loneliness. The schemes and approaches they use range from remarkably simple to technologically sophisticated. Almost any service, charity, or form of merchandise can be the basis for a scam. Some of the most frequent scams involve phony dating sites, ticket vendors, scholarship programs, online games, shopping sites, and charitable groups, just to name a few. An unsolicited email from a foreign student might seek a person's bank account number, supposedly to make a large emergency deposit. A fake shopping website might resemble that of a well-known retailer. A photograph of an impoverished child shared on social media might be the hook for a fraudulent charity pitch. A celebrity video on YouTube might lure viewers to click on a bogus hyperlink promising free gifts. Not only do such schemes hit victims in the pocketbook, they also make people leery of doing business or making donations on legitimate sites.

The growth of online scams has led to an industry dedicated to stopping them. Cybersecurity firms and software makers strive to keep up with the latest tech associated with phishing ploys and data theft. Security experts advise businesses on how to detect and foil online scams. Books and podcasts provide guidance to help individual users avoid scams and identity theft. At the same time, local and federal law enforcement work to foil scammers on the internet and social media. Government websites like FBI.gov offer advice about internet safety and scams, including descriptions of the latest schemes. The Internet Crime Complaint Center (IC3) enables users to report cyber scams to the FBI.

Despite all these efforts, the problem of online scams continues to grow. Ben Herzberg, head of threat research for the internet security firm Imperva, does not expect scams like the bogus *Fortnite* sites to disappear anytime soon. "Basically, cybercriminals are always trying to make money," says Herzberg. "It just works so well, why stop?"[3]

> "Basically, cybercriminals are always trying to make money. It just works so well, why stop?"[3]
>
> —Ben Herzberg, head of threat research for internet security firm Imperva

CHAPTER ONE

The Growing Problem of Online Scams

On May 7, 2019, Baltimore's city government computers shut down. Hackers had attacked the city's computer systems with ransomware, a software that encrypts data and makes it inaccessible. In a note to the city, the hackers demanded payment of three bitcoins (a cyber currency) per computer system, or a total of about $76,000, in exchange for an encryption key to unlock the systems and get them working again. "We've [been] watching you for days," said the ransom note, "and we've worked on your systems to gain full access to your company and bypass all of your protections."[4] The hackers even offered to unlock a few computers as a demonstration to show that they were "honest."

Baltimore officials agonized about what to do. They consulted the FBI and other cybersecurity experts. According to Sheryl Goldstein, the mayor's deputy chief of staff for operations, federal investigators advised against paying the ransom, saying there was less than a fifty-fifty chance of getting the data back even if the hackers were paid off. In the end Baltimore refused to pay and instead hired technicians to repair the locked-up computer systems. "We're not going to pay criminals for bad deeds," said Mayor Bernard C. Young. "That's not going to happen."[5] However, the city's decision proved costly. A little over a month after the ransomware attack, Baltimore's city government had spent more than $18 million to deal with the fallout. The costs included restoring the data, purchasing secure new hardware, and paying for lost revenue due to the attack. The ransomware attack in Baltimore shows how the economic damage from online scams can spiral out of control.

Skyrocketing Losses from Online Scams

Losses due to online scams are skyrocketing. The FBI's 2018 Internet Crime Report found that consumers in the United States lost $7.45 billion in online scams from 2014 to 2018. According to the IC3, a joint project of the FBI and two other agencies, losses from online scams in the United States rose to $2.7 billion in 2018 alone. This was nearly twice the amount from the previous year. The IC3 received 351,937 complaints of internet-related criminal schemes, a jump of 17 percent from 2017. The largest losses—about $1.3 billion, or almost half of the total—came from phishing scams that involved hacking into business and private email accounts. Many such scams led to identity theft or unauthorized transfer of funds. About twenty thousand people fell victim to these email account scams. Stolen personal data caused $149 million in losses, while identity theft led to losses of another $100 million. More than fifty thousand people were scammed with personal data breaches. About sixteen thousand suffered identity theft from online scams. Other internet scams include fake shopping sites, credit card fraud, denial of service attacks, and various threats from malware, ransomware, and viruses.

> "We've [been] watching you for days and we've worked on your systems to gain full access to your company and bypass all of your protections."[4]
>
> —A note from hackers to Baltimore's city government as part of a ransomware scam

Online scams affect users of all ages. In 2018 about half of all victims were under age fifty, accounting for 57 percent of cybercrime losses. Nearly one out of four scam victims was age sixty or older, but young people are far from immune to online scams. The Federal Trade Commission (FTC) found that people who are age thirty-nine and under are 25 percent more likely to report losing

Victim Losses from Online Scams, 2019

Online scams are hugely profitable for cybercriminals—and, in this regard, 2019 proved to be no different. According to the data site Statista, victims of online scams suffered billions of dollars in losses in 2019. The most costly types of cybercrimes were business email compromise and email access compromise. Aside from that, online confidence scams and romance scams alone accounted for $475 million in reported losses to victims.

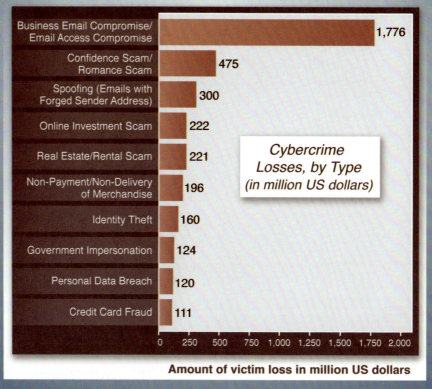

Cybercrime Losses, by Type (in million US dollars)

Type	Amount
Business Email Compromise/Email Access Compromise	1,776
Confidence Scam/Romance Scam	475
Spoofing (Emails with Forged Sender Address)	300
Online Investment Scam	222
Real Estate/Rental Scam	221
Non-Payment/Non-Delivery of Merchandise	196
Identity Theft	160
Government Impersonation	124
Personal Data Breach	120
Credit Card Fraud	111

Amount of victim loss in million US dollars

Source: J. Clement, "Cyber Crime with the Highest Amount of Victim Losses in 2019, by Type," *Statista*, March 27, 2020. www.statista.com.

money to online fraud than people over forty. From August 2017 to August 2019, millennials—those born from 1981 to 1996—lost $450 million in online scams. This total included $70 million in losses due to buying fraudulent merchandise or items that were never delivered. Teens, with less money to spend, reported lower amounts of losses but still were frequent victims of online scams. Overall, in 2018 website scams soared past phone fraud as the number one source of scams that caused people to lose money.

Online Shopping Scams

The growth of online shopping presents many opportunities for con artists and scammers. According to the website eMarketer, consumers in the United States spent more than $580 billion online in 2019, an increase of 14 percent over the previous year. Thus, it is not surprising that online shopping scams are the most common form of internet fraud. In 2018 the Better Business Bureau (BBB) received nearly 10,500 reports of online purchase scams. Doubtless there were many more that went unreported. Online shopping scams are also more likely to be successful than other approaches. The BBB says that 47 percent of consumers exposed to these schemes end up losing money. Certain types of phony shopping websites—such as those dealing in cosmetics, clothing or jewelry, or event tickets—have even higher success rates of more than 80 percent.

Scams aimed at online shoppers range from sales of collectibles and concert tickets to electronics and used cars. In general, scammers take advantage of online shoppers' trust in legitimate sellers to perpetrate their fraud. After sailing through credit card purchases on Amazon or other popular sites for online commerce, shoppers are less likely to pause and scrutinize similar websites. Scam artists employ sophisticated graphics to create fake shopping websites that closely resemble trusted online retailers. The fake sites offer the most popular items at huge discounts, sometimes more than 50 percent. They also tend to add perks such as free shipping, overnight delivery, and coupons for further savings. In their zeal for a bargain, shoppers often fail to see that the offer is too good to be true. "It pays to be very careful when you are shopping online," says Sue McConnell, president of the Cleveland, Ohio, BBB. "If you're Googling the name of a product, for example, you're going to find a website that's probably selling that product at a very low price."[6]

Some bogus retail websites do deliver actual merchandise to customers. Often these are third-rate knockoffs with shoddy workmanship, such as luxury watches that do not keep time or fake designer garments that come apart at the seams. Lots of phony websites never send anything at all and simply pocket the payments. The worst offenders seed their websites, apps, or pop-up ads with malware that can infiltrate the customer's computer and aid in identity theft.

Losses from online shopping scams average about $100. However, one scam that tends to bilk customers for larger sums is selling pets online. Bogus websites hawking puppies, kittens, birds, and exotic animals have some of the highest rates of success. According to the 2018 BBB Scam Tracker Risk Report, phony online pet sales squeeze customers for a median loss of nearly $600 per purchase. In their enthusiasm to replace a lost pet or obtain a special breed, people often ignore warning signs of trouble. Such individuals are liable to make rash decisions they will later regret.

Scam artists use sophisticated graphics to create fake shopping websites that closely resemble those of trusted online retailers like Amazon.

The Rise of Confidence Scams Online

Another major area of online scams is the confidence trick. This goes back to one of the oldest criminal schemes in the world. A "con man" was originally a "confidence man," seeking to gain a victim's trust, or confidence, to scam the person out of money or property. The con artist, male or female, takes advantage of a person's loneliness, sympathy, insecurity, poor health, or ignorance about finance. Online con artists might lie about some great opportunity to make a large sum of money with just a small loan or investment. Some claim a desperate need for funds to help a friend or relative in danger. Some con artists fool victims into giving up personal information, such as a Social Security number or bank account number. Confidence tricks have proved to be easy to adapt to the anonymous communications of email, text messages, and online forums.

One of the most profitable variations is the scam based on online dating websites and people seeking romance. These scammers, claiming to live far away or in a foreign country, play on victims' feelings to get cash. They might insist they need money in an emergency or to purchase a plane ticket to visit in person. Some romance scammers operate in networks. In August 2019 federal investigators announced indictments of eighty people for theft of at least $46 million in a wide-ranging scheme related to online dating. The defendants scammed lonely people, many of them elderly, who were seeking a romantic connection online. "We believe this is one of the largest cases of its kind in U.S. history," says US Attorney Nick Hanna. "We are taking a major step to disrupt these criminal networks."[7]

Typical is the story of a Japanese woman who met a man online claiming to be a captain in the US Army. In the course of ten months of emails, he convinced her he desperately needed money to smuggle himself and several friends out of Syria. The woman ended up sending him $200,000 before discovering the whole story was a fake. Like other victims, she was left feeling angry and depressed at the deception.

According to the FTC, romance-related scams result in more losses than any other form of online fraud. In 2018 alone, the FTC received more than twenty-one thousand complaints about romance scams, an increase of twelve thousand from 2015. These scams were profitable for the con artists, costing victims more than $143 million. Older victims tended to lose the most cash, with those age seventy and over reporting a median loss of $10,000. For such low-tech schemes online, the romance cons are effective. As cybersecurity expert Nathan Wenzler notes, "These kinds of romance scams are very targeted social engineering [psychological manipulation] attacks, effectively 'hacking' the victim's emotions, rather than trying to perform a technical assault."[8]

> "These kinds of romance scams are very targeted social engineering attacks, effectively 'hacking' the victim's emotions, rather than trying to perform a technical assault."[8]
>
> —Nathan Wenzler, a cybersecurity expert

New Wrinkles on an Old Scam

Romance scams are related to one of the classic confidence scams on the internet: the so-called Nigerian prince scam. The ruse—also called 419, for the section of Nigeria's criminal code dealing with fraud—entices victims to pay small amounts of cash up front in exchange for a promise of millions later. In its classic form, the scammer poses as a person of wealth or royalty whose fortune is tied up due to war, corruption, or political turmoil. Via email, the scammer pretends to require the victim's bank account number in order to transfer the money out of the country. If the victim bites, his or her bank account can be drained of funds in short order. Sometimes the request is for small advance payments, purportedly to cover bribes or bank fees, that will supposedly lead to large payouts for the person being scammed. Victims sometimes make several payments before realizing they have been had. Although Nigeria remains a hotbed of online scams, these cons emanate from many different countries today.

Today Nigerian email scammers employ a great deal of research and preparation to increase their profits. Instead of exclusively targeting individuals, they also aim their scams at small businesses. The scammers begin by peppering a company with phishing emails tailored to look like business messages. They need only one employee to click on a link to infiltrate the company's computer system with malware. Once they obtain access, the scammers spend days or weeks doing surveillance on the company's business. The goal is to determine who signs off on purchases and other money transactions. Then they might begin sending this person fake invoices to pay. Sometimes they make a brazen request for the company's letterhead template to aid in

Puppy Scams

In her search for a second dog, Sandy Dowden consulted an online directory of breeders called Puppy Find. There she came across a breeder selling a Cavalier King Charles spaniel, just the type of dog she wanted. The breeder replied to Dowden's email with a number of questions about her home and experience with caring for dogs. "They made it sound like they were really interested in whether or not it would be a good home for the puppy and everything," Dowden recalled.

The sale price of $800 was roughly half of what other breeders wanted. Dowden became leery when she was asked to pay via a money transfer from Walmart. Nonetheless, after the breeder's reassuring emails, Dowden paid the money. Then she waited in vain for the puppy to arrive. Finally, when the breeder demanded an additional $900 for shipping costs, she knew for certain she had been scammed.

Between 2016 and 2018, the BBB tallied ten thousand complaints about so-called puppy scams—which include many other kinds of pets, such as cats, birds, and tortoises. Like Dowden, pet shoppers stumble onto fraudulent sites during a web search. Typically, they pay too much to begin with, then receive demands for more money to get delivery. "I think anybody that goes looking online for a puppy, if you look at more than one or two places, you're going to run across a fraud site," says Steven Baker, an investigator for the BBB. "It's that bad."

Quoted in Jane Lytvynenko, "Scammers Are Tricking People into Buying Puppies That Don't Exist," BuzzFeed News, January 9, 2019. www.buzzfeednews.com.

the scam. They can even doctor genuine invoices from vendors or clients to redirect payments to their own bank.

According to estimates from the FBI, there were more than forty thousand of these business email scams worldwide from October 2013 to December 2016. Losses from the incidents are estimated at more than $5.3 billion, making the more detailed approach very profitable. "[The scammers are] not very technically sophisticated, they can't code, they don't do a lot of automation," says James Bettke, a cyberthreat researcher at Secureworks, which tracks Nigerian email scams, "but their strengths are social engineering and creating agile scams. They spend months sifting through inboxes. They're quiet and methodical."[9]

More Sophisticated Phishing Scams

Whether used in confidence scams or ransomware ploys like the one in Baltimore, phishing is the technological tool of choice for many online scammers. In a typical phishing attack, a spam email arrives urging the recipient to click on a link. Doing so installs malware on the user's computer, from which the scammer can locate personal and financial information or gain access to a larger network. In 2016 the Democratic National Committee (DNC) fell victim to one of the most famous phishing scams in recent years. The attack successfully breached the Gmail account of John Podesta, chair of Hillary Clinton's US presidential campaign. Podesta received an email apparently from Google advising him that he needed to make a password change for security purposes. Podesta consulted a DNC tech expert, but the expert's urgent warning *not* to key in the password got garbled. As a result, Podesta entered the password, providing suspected Russian hackers with the means to infiltrate the system. From this and other phishing attacks, the hackers were able to download a huge trove of emails belonging to Podesta and the DNC, emails that eventually became public and led to embarrassing revelations during the run-up to the election.

The scam perpetrated on Podesta and the DNC was a targeted form of phishing called spear phishing. In this variation, hack-

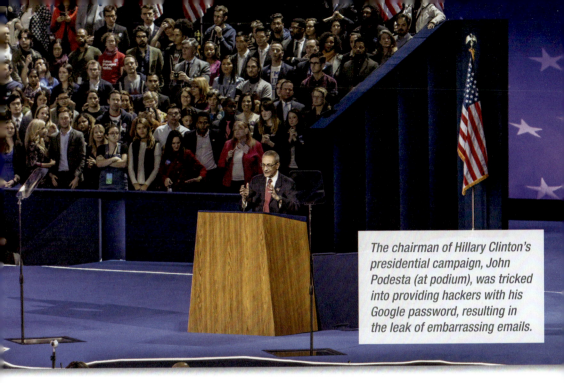

The chairman of Hillary Clinton's presidential campaign, John Podesta (at podium), was tricked into providing hackers with his Google password, resulting in the leak of embarrassing emails.

ers do their homework on a business or organization so they can tailor their phishing emails to the user. When a person receives an email apparently sent by a colleague or client, he or she is more likely to click on an embedded link without a second thought.

Hackers now are using an even more deceptive version of spear phishing called clone phishing. In this scam hackers copy a genuine, previously delivered email and replace its links with a new link or attachment that is coded to deliver malware. There is even a "big fish" form of attack known as whale phishing, in which only the chief officers of a company are targeted. "Fraudsters take months to research these high VIPs, their contacts and their trusted sources," says Riya Sander, who writes about cybersecurity and internet marketing. "Since they target senior managements, the business losses can be huge, which makes whaling attacks more dangerous."[10]

"Fraudsters take months to research these high VIPs, their contacts and their trusted sources. Since they target senior managements, the business losses can be huge, which makes whaling attacks more dangerous."[10]

—Riya Sander, a writer on cybersecurity and internet marketing

19

In 2019 phishing scams produced startling financial losses. IBM says the average phishing-related data breach cost $3.86 million. According to FBI reports, scams that compromised business emails produced a total of about $12 billion in losses. And the problem continues to grow. Attempts at phishing scams increased 65 percent over 2018, with 76 percent of businesses claiming to have been victimized by a phishing attack. Small businesses spent an average of $500 on cybersecurity products to prevent phishing scams.

A Wide Range of Online Scams

The number of successful online scams continues to grow each year, with annual financial losses for individuals and businesses

---

A Spear Phishing Scam in Florida

A recent online scam in Ocala, Florida, shows how brazen spear phishing attacks are becoming in the United States. In September 2019 a senior accountant with the city received a typical business email from a familiar source, Ausley Construction. Ausley was a lead contractor in a construction project for a new terminal at the Ocala International Airport. The email, supposedly from an accounting specialist at Ausley, included a request to change Ausley's bank account information. It provided an official city form with a new routing and account number, plus a copy of a voided check on the account. On October 18, the city paid the regular invoice Ausley submitted for the airport project, amounting to $640,000. However, payment went to the fraudulent account. Four days later, when Ausley contacted the city about not having received the payment, Ocala officials discovered the scam.

In its investigation, the city discovered that the Ausley employee whose name was on the phony email had left the company and claimed not to have sent the message. The email address was slightly different from Ausley's legitimate account and had been set up on September 1. Ocala employees had no idea how the scammers had obtained vendor numbers and other data necessary to perpetrate the scam. "Criminals wake up every morning trying to figure out how to do these things," says Ocala city manager John Zobler. "It's up to us to be vigilant and come up with ways to avoid it from happening."

Quoted in Carlos E. Medina, "Ocala Gets Scammed in 'Spear Phishing' Attack," Ocala.com, October 24, 2019. www.ocala.com.

mounting into billions of dollars. Online scams range from low-tech confidence schemes to high-tech phishing attacks. Scammers set up bogus shopping websites to trick customers into buying worthless merchandise or surrendering credit card numbers. They use romance sites and dating apps to swindle users by appealing to their emotions of sympathy or loneliness. More sophisticated online scams involving spear phishing and malware attacks can empty a person's bank account or cost businesses huge sums. A ransomware attack like the one in Baltimore can virtually paralyze a city government and require enormous expenditures to restore security. With the business of daily life increasingly conducted online, experts say scams are certain to spread. According to Anja Solum, project manager for security firm ADT, "As long as these types of scams keep working, people will continue to use them."[11]

> "As long as these types of [online] scams keep working, people will continue to use them."[11]
>
> —Anja Solum, project manager for security firm ADT

CHAPTER TWO

How Victims Are Harmed by Online Scams

Lisa Bryant, a forty-nine-year-old program manager for an aerospace company, thinks of herself as a savvy consumer. Before making a purchase online, she always does her homework. While browsing the online marketplace Craigslist one day, Bryant noticed a Tahoe deck boat just like the one she and her husband had been looking for. She at once checked out the seller's website, which claimed to run transactions from a warehouse not far from Bryant's home in Tacoma, Washington. "It's a great website. It's very sophisticated," she says. "It makes it look like they have been in business forever. It had references. It had reviews and listed all the locations."[12] The professional look of the website lulled Bryant into ignoring warning signs, such as its lack of listing on the consumer site Yelp and a wire transfer of the purchase amount that initially failed to go through. When Bryant finally did send her payment to the company's bank account, she received nothing in return. No boat was delivered, and the seller's website had disappeared. Efforts to get her bank to cancel the payment were not successful. For her trouble, Bryant lost $16,400. She and thousands like her continue to suffer financial losses and other harms from online scams.

Danger of Financial Ruin

Losses from online scams can vary widely, from less than one hundred dollars to alarming sums in the hundreds of thousands. More affluent victims like Bryant and her husband can chalk up a significant loss to experience and move on. But lower-income people can face financial ruin from an online scam. One disastrous transaction can be the difference between paying the rent or facing eviction. BBB statistics show that those with annual incomes of less than $50,000 are more likely to fall for scammers via email, social media, or bogus shopping websites than are upper-income individuals.

Scammers are constantly adding new wrinkles to confuse their victims. In August 2019 a Nashville man fell for a scheme involving pop-up ads and gift cards. First he received a pop-up ad on his computer with the message "your connection has been compromised."[13] Later he got a phone call from a scammer who claimed to work for Microsoft's security unit. The man was told that his credit cards had been tapped for thousands of dollars in fraudulent charges. The scammer told him he had to pay off the balances with gift cards before the company could investigate. "They're like, 'no sir, we're not scamming you, we're just looking into this. Again, all this money will be returned to you in 72 hours,'"[14] recalls Sergeant Michael Warren of the Metro Nashville Police Department's fraud unit. The victim withdrew cash to buy $34,000 worth of Target gift cards, then passed along the card numbers and PINs to the scammer. Employees at the victim's bank and at Target tried to stop him, but he was convinced he had to follow the scammer's orders. The victim's losses amounted to half of his life savings.

> "They're like, 'no sir, we're not scamming you, we're just looking into this. Again, all this money will be returned to you in 72 hours.'"[14]
>
> —Michael Warren, a sergeant in the Metro Nashville Police Department's fraud unit

Along with financial disaster, there can be feelings of shock, fear, and frustration. A woman in Mount Pleasant, South Carolina, also fell victim to the gift card scam. A female claiming to be from Apple Support called to warn her that her computer's IP address had been compromised and her bank and credit card accounts

Statistics show that people who make less than $50,000 per year are victimized more often than wealthier people, and are more likely to face financial ruin as a consequence of being scammed.

were in danger. The caller ID matched the phone number on Apple's website, convincing her the call was genuine. The caller also knew her personal information, including Social Security number, banking information, and credit card numbers plus the credit limits. She was told that all her money was at risk and she needed to buy gift cards loaded with large amounts at several stores in order to protect herself. "Everything you say, they have an answer, everything you propose, they have something to counter it," she says. "I was very frustrated and flustered and shocked. I was frightened to death."[15] She purchased dozens of gift cards and provided the caller with the numbers. Two days later, when she called Apple, she was told that they had no fraud department and that she had been scammed. Altogether, she lost her life savings of $64,000—not to mention the emotional turmoil she had to endure.

Mount Pleasant police inspector Chip Googe admitted there was little the local police could do. "They know enough about you to make it seem like it's real, whether they know the last four [digits] of your social, they know the names of your children, all these things that can be found on social media or other online ways," he says. "It makes you feel comfortable to where you think you're talking to someone from a legitimate company when, in fact, you're talking to someone who may not even be in the country."[16]

> "Everything you say, they have an answer, everything you propose, they have something to counter it. I was very frustrated and flustered and shocked. I was frightened to death."[15]
>
> —A woman in Mount Pleasant, South Carolina, who fell victim to a gift card scam

Health Dangers from Online Scams

Some online scammers not only take victims' money, they can also endanger their health. According to the US Food and Drug Administration (FDA), bogus online pharmacies operate without regard for laws and regulations. Many offer prescription medicines at deep discounts and do not require that customers have a valid prescription. Often these rogue pharmacy sites are selling medicines that are counterfeit or unapproved for safe use. The medicines may contain too much or too little of the active ingredient needed to treat a disease or health condition. They might have been stored improperly at the wrong temperature or contain the wrong formula or harmful additives. Taking pills purchased from unlicensed online pharmacies could lead to dangerous side effects or serious allergic reactions.

The same warnings pertain to buying diet supplements, medical devices, health foods, and cosmetics online. Frequently, these

Scamming Small Businesses

Small businesses often operate on thin margins, meaning that a sizable loss from an internet scam can place the whole enterprise in peril. According to the BBB, successful online scams cost small businesses more than $50,000 on average. "Scams are a significant—and growing—problem for small businesses," says Beverly Baskin, interim president and chief executive officer of the Council of Better Business Bureaus. "Nearly two-thirds of those we surveyed said their business had been targeted by a scammer in the past three years, and many said their businesses suffered a loss of consumer trust as a result." Small business owners, more than half of whom are age fifty or older, have learned to keep a wary eye out for cyber scammers.

Small businesses are subject to the same types of phishing schemes as individuals are. Scammers frequently try to gain control of small business bank accounts via malware or data theft. They may also pose as government agents threatening to suspend a business license or impose fines if the owner does not pay bogus fees or taxes. Another frequent ploy is to invoice a business owner for supplies he or she never ordered. Scams associated with tech support often target small businesses. In these scams, the business receives an email or pop-up message warning that its computers have been compromised and an expensive security patch is needed to fix the problem. A harried business owner, concerned about the expense of a shutdown, may agree to pay a suspicious bill too readily.

Quoted in Kenneth Terrell, "Scams Are a Growing Threat, Small Business Owners Say," AARP, July 6, 2018. www.aarp.org.

---

websites or apps use promotional phrases such as "no risk," "quick results," "scientific breakthrough," or "money-back guarantee" to attract customers. Health experts warn online shoppers to beware of internet pharmacies or health websites that advertise incredibly low prices or claim to ship worldwide. Often, these are telltale signs of a scam. And like other rogue websites, online pharmacies may also take shoppers' money without sending anything in return.

Online marketing of marijuana and cannabis products is also rife with fraud. To begin with, sending marijuana through the mail is illegal in the United States. This applies to pot used for either recreational or medical purposes. Nonetheless, fraudulent websites persist. Some sites scam customers out of their money without delivering the product. Others sell marijuana that is infused with synthetic chemicals or contains widely varying levels of THC, the psychoactive ingredient that creates the user's high. States where pot is legal have regulations that ensure the product is safe, pure, and accurately labeled. Online scammers seek to evade these regulations and do business by mail anyway. Legitimate marketers say customers who buy pot online could be endangering their health. "Anywhere you go to, even if it's California or Colorado, they should be able to tell where [the marijuana is] from, where it was planted, when it was planted, the lot number, what kind it is," says Da'Quan Myers, owner of a CBD store in Fayetteville, Arkansas. (CBD stands for cannabidiol, one of the active ingredients in marijuana.) According to Myers, buying online is "like taking a chance getting it off the street. That's scary."[17]

Even more dangerous are internet pharmacies that break the law prohibiting online sales of opioids. In June 2018 the FDA issued warnings to a total of fifty-three websites, ordering them to stop illegally marketing opioids online, including oxycodone and tramadol. The FDA warned that patients who turn to illegal online pharmacies to purchase any prescription medicines may be putting their lives at risk. The unregulated drugs can be counterfeit, contaminated with other substances, expired, or misbranded. Donald D. Ashley, director of the Office of Compliance in the FDA's Center for Drug Evaluation and Research, notes:

> The public needs to know that no one is authorized to sell or distribute opioids via the internet in the U.S., with or without a prescription. Drug dealers and rogue website operators are using the internet to fuel the opioid crisis, heartlessly targeting millions of Americans struggling with opioid use disorder. We will continue to aggressively pursue these criminals and take swift action to protect the American public.[18]

Hassles of Medical Record Theft

Another online scam related to personal health involves the theft of medical records. Scammers who use phishing schemes to break into doctors' computer systems are generally seeking patient information for use in identity theft. Stolen medical records are especially valuable to cyberthieves. Personal data such as Social Security numbers or bank account numbers sell for less than $50 on the dark web or black market. However, health insurance numbers and medical records bring more than $1,000 per person. Older patients are special targets, since their medical information can be used for fraudulent billing of Medicare. According to the AARP, Medicare pays out $60 billion each year in billing scams.

Theft of medical records also creates lifelong headaches for patients who are victimized. Frank Abagnale, a fraud expert at the AARP, tells the story of five-year-old Gavin Karpinsky, whose Social Security number, insurance information, and other personal

Scammers use phishing techniques to break into the medical records kept by doctors and other health care providers.

data was stolen in a hacking attack on his doctor's computers. Gavin began receiving bills in the mail for nutrition products sold via a TV informercial. A larger problem for Gavin's family, however, will be dealing with the fallout going forward. "I was told his information will continue to be sold on the black market and his medical identity can continue to be used," says Gavin's mother, Heather. "He's 5—he shouldn't really have a credit report or a credit rating."[19] Abagnale notes that Gavin's credit and medical data will have to be monitored closely for the rest of his life.

> "I was told his information will continue to be sold on the black market and his medical identity can continue to be used. He's 5—he shouldn't really have a credit report or a credit rating."[19]
>
> —Heather Karpinsky, whose son's medical records were hacked

Once personal medical records are stolen, adult patients can find themselves at the mercy of scammers. Information that might create a negative stigma, such as an abortion or treatment for cancer or a sexually transmitted disease, exists in the dark recesses of the internet basically forever. Patients can be targeted for blackmail to keep their records from reaching their employer or family members. There are also potential health risks if a person's medical records become tainted. A scammer might use the victim's stolen ID to get medical care, with the imposter's information ending up on the victim's records. "If you are in an accident and rushed to the emergency room, doctors retrieving your electronic record could see the wrong blood type or not know that you are allergic to certain medications, or that you have a pre-existing condition," says business reporter Gail Buckner. "This could lead to misdiagnosis or mistreatment, with potentially deadly consequences."[20]

Emotional Impact of Being Scammed

In addition to financial problems, online scams also cause severe emotional effects. Falling victim to an online scam can leave people traumatized much as if they had been physically attacked.

In addition to financial losses, the victims of online scams often suffer from severe emotional trauma.

Marv and Penny Wasser, an elderly couple in Spokane, Washington, were ensnared by a fraud ring fronted by a man posing as a detective with the Los Angeles Police Department. The scammers set up fake online banking accounts in the Wassers' name using stolen personal data. The bogus detective then warned the couple they were being targeted by scam artists, and he directed them to wire money to offshore accounts to protect themselves. The Wassers not only lost $500,000, which was their entire life savings, they also experienced severe emotional damage. "It's devastating," admits Penny. "It's embarrassing. It's heartbreaking."[21] She and her husband have struggled to overcome their feelings of anxiety and depression. "You really wish

> "It's devastating. It's embarrassing. It's heartbreaking."[21]
>
> —Penny Wasser, on the emotional toll of losing one's life savings in an online scam

you'd die," says Marv. "I should have been smart enough not to get into our deep savings."[22] The Wassers relied on help from friends and neighbors to get back on their feet.

Like the Wassers, people who are victimized by internet scams can be overcome by a range of negative emotions. There is shame and embarrassment from having been fooled by a fraudulent scheme. There is guilt at having lost family funds and put loved ones at risk. There can also be a larger loss of trust in general, leading to paranoid fears about falling for another scam. Those who succumb to a dating site swindle may be reluctant to enter into romantic relationships. For many victims the impact of a costly online scam can persist for years. Stephen Pedneault, a

Exploiting a Health Crisis

The email bore an eye-opening header: "Singapore Specialist: Corona Virus Safety Measures." The full message read: "Go through the attached document on safety measures regarding the spreading of corona virus. This little measure can save you. . . . Use the link below to download." Once the link was clicked, the user suddenly had a big problem with another kind of virus. Malware invaded his or her computer, along with the danger of stolen data, identity theft, and financial losses.

Thousands of computers received this spam email and others like it in late January 2020, just as news reports about the deadly novel coronavirus, or COVID-19, were sounding the alarm. Since online scammers routinely try to take advantage of people's fear and anxiety, a major health-related threat like coronavirus makes a perfect theme for a phishing attack. "Unfortunately, we see this often in geopolitical events and world events," says Francis Gaffney, the director of threat intelligence at Mimecast, an email security company. "This is when cybercriminals seek opportunities to use the confusion that vulnerable people have." During a health crisis, people have many questions and concerns, and they naturally turn to sources that claim to have answers. As Gaffney notes, "So if you say 'Coronavirus is now more prevalent!' people are going to think 'Oh my gosh, it's more contagious than has been reported in the news.' . . . And they're more likely to click on links, because they are concerned."

Quoted in Lily Hay Newman, "Watch Out for Coronavirus Phishing Scams," *Wired*, January 31, 2020. www.wired.com.

forensic accountant in Glastonbury, Connecticut, has dealt with many fraud victims. He believes there needs to be more emphasis on dealing with victims' anger and emotional trauma. As Pednault acknowledges, "Someone who is stable today could be very unstable tomorrow."[23]

Societal Cost of Online Scams

People who fall for online scams can suffer harm in many ways. In most cases, financial losses represent the chief impact on victims. Losses can range from small sums to several hundred thousand dollars, sometimes draining victims of their life savings. Internet scams such as fraudulent online pharmacies and sites that market illegal drugs also can endanger people's health. Hacking and theft of personal data, including confidential medical files, not only place patients' credit at risk but can lead to tainted records due to health insurance scams. Often forgotten are the psychological and emotional effects of having been scammed. Negative effects ranging from anger and guilt to paranoid distrust can last for years. All these impacts must be taken into account when reckoning the societal cost of online scams.

CHAPTER THREE

Why People Fall for Online Scams

When Debby Montgomery Johnson lost her husband of twenty-six years to a heart attack, she felt completely adrift. Friends who had met their spouses on dating sites suggested she try online dating. Johnson's first few encounters were hopeless. But then she made contact with a widower from London whose online conversations gave her a feeling of comfort. He described himself as a contractor in the hardwood tree business, with interests in Malaysia and other countries. Johnson, naturally cautious due to her background as a former US Air Force intelligence officer and senior branch manager at a bank, did some checking on the man's background. The company he claimed to work for had never heard of him.

Despite this discovery, Johnson rationalized that everything was probably okay, that it must be a large firm with lots of contractors. Months of intimate exchanges online had convinced her that she and this man had a great deal in common. Then he began to ask for increasingly large sums of money to help with temporary business expenses. Despite some initial doubts, she never refused. Finally one day he said he had something to tell Johnson that was likely to hurt her. "So I was like, 'Eric, are you sure you want to do this?'" she recalls. "And he said yes. That's when he proceeded to say, 'This has all been a scam.'"[24] Even though Johnson made screenshots of the scammer's face and had records of their conversations, FBI agents admitted there was little they could do. The scammer was overseas, and the money had already changed hands. Altogether, Johnson's foray into online romance ended up costing her more than $1 million.

One of the Fastest-Growing Scams

Romance scams like the one Johnson fell for are one of the fastest-growing internet crimes. In 2019 victims reported losses from romance scams of $201 million. The FTC says people reported losing more money to romance scams in 2018 and 2019 than to any other form of fraud. Observers often wonder how someone could be taken in by these schemes. Sometimes the people who are scammed are unaware that online romance scams exist. But even savvy, otherwise careful individuals like Johnson can fall victim to a clever scammer with a talent for playing on a person's emotions. A 2017 study in the United Kingdom found that better-educated people are more likely to get entangled in romance scams. Overconfidence seems to make people more vulnerable. Moreover, when romantic feelings are involved, people want to believe in the scenario even if red flags are warning them that something is not right.

Scammers go to great lengths to create elaborate fake profiles on dating sites and apps. They also target victims via social media sites, including Google Hangouts, Instagram, and Facebook. They constantly troll for people's weaknesses. In Johnson's case, she had just lost her husband and was seeking companionship. As Amy Fontinelle of the investor website the Ascent explains, "Romance scammers create online dating profiles designed to lure people who are at their most vulnerable: those in a period of transition. So they make realistic profiles pretending to be widows or widowers looking to find love again, or they say they've recently lost a parent or child. These backstories create the perfect way to 'bond' with a target."[25]

Once they have made contact, romance scammers will soften up their targets by talking or messaging several times each

> "Romance scammers create online dating profiles designed to lure people who are at their most vulnerable: those in a period of transition. . . . These backstories create the perfect way to 'bond' with a target."[25]
>
> —Amy Fontinelle, a writer for the investor website the Ascent

Scammers sometimes use online dating websites to find victims who are lonely and vulnerable to emotional manipulation.

day. According to investigators at the FTC, scammers will usually claim to be living or working outside the United States, often as an oil worker, medical staffer, salesperson, or military official. "Scammers perform these cons for a living, so they're often quite efficient," notes Fontinelle. "They use scripts that save them time composing messages and help them keep their fake stories straight."[26]

Having established a relationship of trust, scammers will then ask the victim for money. The need is always urgent, whether it is to pay for a plane ticket, surgery, gambling debts, custom fees, a passport or visa, or some other emergency. The targeted person is told to wire payments to a designated account or buy gift cards and send along their numbers. These methods enable the scammer to get the cash quickly without it being traceable. When the victim becomes suspicious, the scammer will break off contact and disappear. Like Johnson, victims can be blindsided with enormous financial losses and emotional pain. Yet more and more people fall prey to such schemes every day.

Romance Scams and Money Mules

Some victims of romance scams are so thoroughly taken in that they end up participating in criminal activity. In August 2019 the FBI's IC3 issued warnings about a new tactic used by romance scammers. After meeting lovelorn men or women on dating sites, they not only bilk them out of their savings but also recruit them as so-called money mules to launder drug money or other illegal funds. Typically, the scam artists direct their smitten targets to open bank accounts, purportedly to send or receive sums of cash. "These accounts are used to facilitate criminal activities for a short period of time," says the FBI. "If the account is flagged by the financial institution, it may be closed and the actor will either direct the victim to open a new account or begin grooming a new victim." According to the BBB, nearly 30 percent of those caught in romance scams are also used as money mules.

A few people go even further to cooperate with their online lovers. In 2014 an Australian grandmother named Maria Elvira Pinto Exposto was arrested at a Malaysian airport carrying a backpack of clothes with more than 2.2 pounds (1 kg) of crystal meth. Exposto explained that the bag of meth was intended for a man she had been dating online. Supposedly, he was an American soldier. Exposto spent five years in jail and narrowly avoided death by hanging (the penalty in Malaysia for drug trafficking). Her sentence was overturned in November 2019.

Quoted in Tomas Foltyn, "FBI Warns of Romance Scams Using Online Daters as Money Mules," We Live Security, August 7, 2019. www.welivesecurity.com.

Taking Advantage of Vulnerabilities

Different types of online scams appeal to particular emotions to hook their victims. A yearning for romance and emotional connection can make a person ripe for an online dating scam. Greed can induce people to hand over their money to a stranger in anticipation of a large payoff later. Fear can cause people to fall for tech support scams that claim to make their computers more secure. Feelings of sympathy can prompt people to make payments they cannot afford to bogus charities. Loneliness can lead isolated individuals to trust internet or phone scammers simply because they seem kind and concerned. Successful online scammers use their expertise to take advantage of each victim's most vulnerable spots.

Online scams also succeed by developing a professional look. They mimic the websites of established companies or enhance their visual appeal with high-quality graphics and photographs. Scammers may claim to have impressive credentials from a university or government agency. Email or social media scammers might use buzzwords from a profession to make themselves seem legitimate. The key is to gain the target's confidence.

Another way that scammers seek to establish trust quickly is by using the victim's personal information. For example, a bit of research online can produce the names of a person's grandchildren or other relatives. Then the scammer might call, imitating a police officer or hospital official, with news that a grandchild has been involved in an accident and needs immediate funds for medical care. An elderly person is likely to wire money at once from a sense of panic.

Falling for Tech Support Scams

The elderly are often targeted in tech support online scams. This is because many elderly people lack experience with home computers or mobile devices. They are more likely to be spooked by a message about computer viruses and malware. Scammers posing as technicians can easily exploit older people's limited knowl-

Elderly people, who often lack experience with computers and mobile devices, are vulnerable to scammers who masquerade as tech support professionals.

edge to convince them that their device is under attack. "There's just an endless amount of fear appeals," says Doug Shadel, lead researcher on consumer fraud for the AARP. "[Scammers] realize that fear sells better than good news."[27]

> "There's just an endless amount of fear appeals. [Scammers] realize that fear sells better than good news."[27]
>
> —Doug Shadel, lead researcher on consumer fraud for the AARP

The scam usually begins with a pop-up warning on a device or an unsolicited phone call. According to the FTC, tech support scammers frequently pose as employees with Apple, Microsoft, or some well-known security software company. They helpfully request remote access to the computer to run a bogus diagnostic test. Inevitably, they will find a virus or malware that will supposedly erase all the stored data or freeze the machine and render it unusable. The victim is then pressured to pay for repairs, replacement software, and other services. The bill will quickly mount into hundreds of dollars. Scammers generally try to charge the payment by credit card number or ask for payment by gift card or money transfer because these methods are harder to trace. In the heat of the moment, victims frequently do not question odd requests for payment, focusing instead on getting the transaction done quickly. In the worst-case scenario, online scammers may use their access to the victim's computer to install genuine malware. This can lead to stolen data and identity theft.

Some older victims are made more vulnerable to online scams due to illness or mental decline. In one case in Washington State, an elderly man was bilked in dozens of security software transactions that totaled nearly $90,000. The victim, a retired doctor, was apparently the target of a network of scammers. The losses were discovered only after his death. In court filings, the man's son wrote, "Under normal circumstances, there was no way that he would have paid multiple thousands of dollars, even once for technical services for his personal computer. . . . However, my father was induced to make these payments after he contracted Parkinson's disease."[28]

Online scammers employ other ruses to instill panic in internet users. Keying in an incorrect URL address can produce a sudden pop-up screen with flashing lights and even blaring audio. The user is urged to clink a link to download antivirus software. The warning comes from a phony cybersecurity company with a name like Spy Wiper or System Defender. Trying to close the web browser fails to delete the screen. Sometimes the entire screen will turn blue, imitating the "blue death" screen familiar to computer users whose machines have crashed. All this is designed to provoke fear, and it is successful all too often. According to the AARP's Fraud Resource Center, "Microsoft has estimated that tech support scams bilk 3.3 million people a year, at an annual cost of $1.5 billion—an average loss of more than $450 per victim. And those numbers are probably on the low side, since many victims never realize they've been conned."[29]

Online scammers try to instill panic in potential victims by causing their computer screens to turn blue and by displaying a message that urges them to click a link that gives the criminals access to the machine's hard drive.

Seduced by Promise of a Big Payoff

Sixty-three-year-old David Carter should have seen the con coming, but the thought of easy money clouded his judgment. In the spring of 2018, the retired Maryland resident with a master's degree in technology thought he had run across a sweet deal. One day he received an email from a Swiss company offering him a non-labor-intensive job at a salary of $100,000. Carter knew that the job market for tech firms was on fire. The deal was just too good to pass up. Beginning in June he began making thousands of dollars in credit card purchases of iPhones and iPads from retailers like Walmart and Best Buy. Then he would send the devices from his Maryland home to a California address. For the first few weeks, the company paid Carter's credit card bill. In July, however, the payments were voided. Carter's bank told him the debts he had accumulated were his responsibility. By this time the Swiss firm's website had vanished. His contacts at the company no longer answered the phone. All of a sudden, having never re-

Youthful Victims of Online Scams

Young people are less desirable targets for online scams since they generally have less money and fewer credit cards. Because they tend to ignore unfamiliar callers, they fall victim to phone scams much less often. Yet a 2016 Microsoft survey found that those aged eighteen to twenty-four were two and a half times more likely than seniors to fall for a tech support scam. When confronted with a fraudulent pop-up alert or email on a computer or mobile device, the young were more apt to pay for a phony software fix or provide bank account information that could lead to theft of funds. They clicked on phishing links more often as well, enabling scammers to gain control of their devices.

Cybersecurity experts say young people may be used to quick fixes for any technical problems that arise. They may also be overconfident about their knowledge of tech security. This may render them more vulnerable to tech support and other online scams. "The takeaway here is simple," says the editor of the website TechAdvisory.org, "Cybersecurity is about more than just firewalls and antivirus software. You *need* to shore up the human side of your protection protocols."

TechAdvisory.org, "Youth: The Real Tech-Scam Victims," November 10, 2016. www.techadvisory.org.

ceived a dime of his promised salary, Carter was on the hook for $80,000.

Online financial scammers frequently target retired seniors because many have large amounts of cash in the bank. "They prefer to pursue 45-to-75-year-old widowed men and women," says Frank T. McAndrew, a psychology professor at Knox College in Galesburg, Illinois. "The thinking goes that this demographic is most likely to have money and be lonely—in other words, easy marks."[30] Nonetheless, anyone can be victimized by these scams. Too often greed causes people to overlook warning signs of trouble. For example, the so-called Nigerian prince or 419 scam depends on the victim being seduced by the promise of a big payoff. In an unsolicited email, scammers claim to need a certain amount of cash quickly in order to get their hands on a fortune, which they are willing to share. The victim need only pay a fraction of the amount up front—as well as turn over bank account information for the eventual money transfer. In the end, no transfer is made, the original payment is lost, and the victim's account may be emptied of funds. Afterward, the duped individual is likely to wonder how he or she could have been so foolish. Yet variations of this scheme net millions for scammers every year.

Exploiting Sympathy and Good Intentions

Online scammers also take advantage of their victims' compassion and good intentions. Many people want to believe that those they correspond with online share their values. They assign qualities to the other person that suit their own views of the world. At the same time, they overestimate their ability to detect a fraud. And once they commit themselves to an online relationship, they are reluctant to change course. To exploit such

> "They prefer to pursue 45-to-75-year-old widowed men and women. The thinking goes that this demographic is most likely to have money and be lonely—in other words, easy marks."[30]
>
> —Frank T. McAndrew, a psychology professor at Knox College in Galesburg, Illinois

feelings, scammers on dating sites or social media gradually establish a bond of trust. As McAndrew explains:

> They utilize the foot-in-the-door technique—a small, innocuous request—to draw their targets in, perhaps something as simple as asking for advice about what to see on vacation in the mark's home country. When victims acquiesce [comply], they begin to perceive themselves as someone who provides help. Through a series of baby steps, they move from doing small favors that cost little to giving away the store.[31]

Another way online scam artists profit from people's generosity and compassion is with charity scams. Some create fake websites designed to look like they are affiliated with well-known charitable groups, such as the Red Cross or Salvation Army. Following major disasters, including earthquakes, floods, wildfires, or hurricanes, charity scams pop up all over the internet. They make urgent requests for donations, siphoning off funds that should be directed to legitimate groups. Phony charity websites also target compassionate visitors with photographs of ill or impoverished children in foreign nations. Other scams seek to exploit sympathy for abandoned or mistreated animals. Scammers depend on their emotional appeals to distract people from inquiring too closely about the fake organization.

People fall for online scams for many reasons. Scammers have certainly become expert at using a variety of means to create plausible scams. They fashion professional-looking fake websites, create detailed phony profiles on dating sites and apps, and employ sophisticated phishing schemes to steal data. However,

> "Unfortunately, consumers overestimate their ability to back out if the offer turns out to be a scam."[32]
>
> —Stacey Wood, a professor of psychology at Scripps College in Claremont, California

scammers also exploit the vulnerability of their victims. People can be fooled by online scams because of greed, vanity, fear, or panic. They can also be exploited because of tech ignorance, illness, loneliness, mental decline, misplaced trust, and feelings of compassion. Much of the success of online scams depends on flawed human beings and their emotional weaknesses. As noted by Stacey Wood, a professor of psychology at Scripps College in Claremont, California, "Unfortunately, consumers overestimate their ability to back out if the offer turns out to be a scam."[32]

CHAPTER FOUR

Can Online Scams Be Stopped?

In her job as a bank teller in Serangoon, Singapore, Sheila Chow strives to help customers however she can. On September 26, 2019, Chow was able to deliver a special service. The incident began when a female customer in her early forties made a request for a money transfer. She wanted to send $1,500 to a personal account overseas. As part of her job, Chow asked the woman about the purpose of the transfer and her relationship with the recipient. "After speaking with the customer for 25 minutes," says Chow, "I realized she was being cheated by a stranger online."[33] Chow discovered that the woman was the victim of an online romance scam. Following weeks of increasingly intimate online chats, the scammer claimed he was trying to send the woman expensive dresses, but the parcel supposedly had been stopped at customs in Singapore. He said he needed $3,500 so that she could receive her package. The woman had already sent the man $2,000 by online transfer when Chow made her discovery. Instead of transferring the second amount, the bank assisted the woman in filing a police report. For their help in foiling the scam, Chow and another bank employee won the Singapore Police Force's Public Spiritedness Award. According to Chow, "We put ourselves in the shoes of the customer, who may have lost her hard-earned money without our intervention."[34]

> "After speaking with the customer for 25 minutes, I realized she was being cheated by a stranger online."[33]
>
> —Sheila Chow, a bank teller in Singapore, on helping foil a romance scam

A Challenge for Law Enforcement

Chow's quick-witted response helped derail one online scammer. However, the parcel scam remains a popular venture in Singapore. Of the 660 internet romance scams reported there in 2019, nearly 60 percent involved parcel scams. Sometimes the scammers pretend to be employees of a courier company or a government agency. If their targets balk at sending the money, the scammers make bogus threats to prosecute them. Victims are often left frightened and intimidated, not knowing where to turn. Like law enforcement elsewhere, police in Singapore struggle to deal with the rise in these online scams. However, investigators occasionally meet with success. In 2018 officers from Singapore, Malaysia, and Hong Kong combined to break up an international syndicate that specialized in online romance scams. The group had hauled in nearly $20 million from its operations in the region. The arrested suspects included sixteen Malaysians, two Nigerian men, and one Chinese woman. Police also seized smartphones, laptops, and ATM cards used in the criminal operation.

In August 2019 Singapore police announced a new Anti-Scam Centre whose focus is to detect and disrupt online scammers and reduce the financial bite on victims. Police are partnering with local banks as part of their campaign to stop online scams. One initiative seeks to speed up the process of freezing scam-related bank accounts after police notification. Banks also agreed to provide the police with bank balances and statements promptly to aid in investigations. "Scammers are moving very fast now with the advent of technology," says Deputy Superintendent of Police Lim Hao Jun. "We have to catch up and be faster than them."[35] In the Anti-Scam Centre's first two months, it dealt with 1,047 cases totaling $2.4 million in potential losses. By freezing more than eight hundred bank accounts, the new center was able to recover more than a third of victims' losses, a

> "Scammers are moving very fast now with the advent of technology. We have to catch up and be faster than them."[35]
>
> —Lim Hao Jun, deputy superintendent of police in Singapore

much higher rate than before. The Singapore police's anti-scam efforts demonstrate how important it is for law enforcement to act swiftly and decisively to stop online scams.

Internet Scams and the FBI

Federal law enforcement in the United States is constantly seeking new ways to stanch the flood of online scam cases. Most attention is focused on national security issues related to cybercrime and hacking by foreign governments, including terrorism. But cases of online fraud and deception are also a priority. Nearly two decades ago, Thomas T. Kubic, then the deputy director of the FBI, appeared before the House Judiciary Committee to explain the challenges of fighting internet crime:

> The very nature of the Internet and the rapid pace of technological change in our society result in otherwise traditional fraud schemes becoming magnified when these tools are utilized as part of the scheme. The Internet presents new and significant investigatory challenges for law enforcement at all levels. These challenges include: the need to track down sophisticated users who commit unlawful acts on the Internet while hiding their identities; the need for close coordination among law enforcement agencies; and the need for trained and well-equipped personnel to gather evidence, investigate, and prosecute these cases.[36]

Around the time of Kubic's testimony, the FBI joined with the National White Collar Crime Center and the Bureau of Justice Assistance to create a central website for reporting suspected cybercrime and online scams. The website, called the Internet Crime Complaint Center (IC3), receives reports from victims of online scams as well as from people reporting on their behalf. Beside digital complaint forms, the site includes information about ongoing investigations, cybercrime prevention tips, and explanations of widely used scams, such as phishing, credit card fraud,

The FBI (whose headquarters in Washington DC is pictured) uses a website called the Internet Crime Complaint Center to receive reports of online scams.

and identify theft. The IC3 has become so well known that scammers have impersonated IC3 investigators in their scams. In 2018 scammers pretending to be with the IC3 emailed victims to tell them their computers had been compromised. The scam artists promised victims more than $2 million in restitution if they would fill out an attached complaint form. Clicking on the link to send the form would then infect the victim's computer with malware.

In 2019 the IC3 received 467,361 complaints involving more than $3.5 billion in losses. Online scams included business email compromise, ransomware, tech support fraud, and elder fraud. In its first year of operation, the IC3's Recovery Asset Team helped in recovering more than $300 million lost in online scams. "We encourage everyone to use IC3 and reach out to their local field office to report malicious activity," says Matt Gorham, assistant director of the FBI's Cyber Division. "Cyber is the ultimate team sport."[37]

Global Efforts to Stop Online Fraud

As online scams have ballooned into a global problem, the FBI has partnered with law enforcement agencies from many countries in the effort to stop cyber criminals. On September 10, 2019, the US Department of Justice announced a massive roundup of digital scammers around the globe. Over a four-month period, more than 281 suspects were arrested in the United States, Nigeria, Japan, France, Italy, the United Kingdom, and four other countries. The scammers were involved in business email compromise (BEC) schemes, sending fake phishing emails to companies' financial officers and payment personnel who perform wire transfers. The scams used social engineering to trick unwary company executives and employees into making wire payments to bank accounts set up by the scammers.

Scammers sometimes try to withdraw money from a victim's bank account. This action can be foiled by two-factor authentication, which helps ensure that the person requesting access is actually the account owner.

Dubbed Operation reWired, the FBI-led effort seized nearly $3.7 million in stolen funds and recovered another $118 million in fraudulent wire transfers. It was the largest coordinated global law enforcement effort ever to disrupt online scam networks. On the US side it included thirty-nine of the FBI's fifty-six field offices and members of local and state law enforcement agencies, as well as the US Department of Homeland Security, US Department of State, US Department of the Treasury, and US Postal Inspection Service. As FBI director Christopher Wray declared, "Through Operation reWired, we're sending a clear message to the criminals who orchestrate these BEC schemes: We'll keep coming after you, no matter where you are. And to the public, we'll keep doing whatever we can to protect you."[38] The operation came one year after federal authorities had pulled off another successful sweep of email scams. Operation Wire Wire, as the 2018 effort was called, nabbed seventy-four suspected cybercrooks and recovered about $14 million in fraudulent wire transfers.

Federal agents warn that scammers are only getting more sophisticated in their online email schemes. The BEC approach foiled by Operation reWired was likely to fool anyone who was not in the habit of double-checking sources. "If you saw the email, it would look very legitimate," says Special Agent Jennifer Boyer, who investigated the case from the FBI's field office in New Haven, Connecticut. Boyer urges those responsible for wiring money for company payments to pause and check all requests before clicking on send. "Take a moment to consider that maybe it's not your boss and pick up the phone and verify," she says. "It's that second factor authentication that people really need to implement, and so many people don't."[39] Two-factor authentication is an extra layer of security designed to

> "Take a moment to consider that maybe it's not your boss and pick up the phone and verify. It's that second factor authentication that people really need to implement, and so many people don't."[39]
>
> —Jennifer Boyer, FBI special agent

VIEWPOINT

Banks Must Help Protect the Elderly from Online Scams

Online scammers prey on the elderly, since many older people have financial assets yet lack experience with computers and email. David Lazarus, a business columnist for the *Los Angeles Times*, believes banks and businesses have a responsibility to help people—and especially the elderly—avoid losing money in online scams and wire fraud rackets.

> It's time for businesses to stop wringing their hands over the aggressiveness and cleverness of scammers, and to be much more assertive in protecting people from fraud—especially seniors.
>
> I say this after speaking with Montrose resident Sal Macaione, 79, who fell victim the other day to what's known as the "grandparent scam." . . . The grandparent scam is particularly insidious because it preys upon older folks' sense of duty. Scammers know that if they say the right words, a senior will hand over almost any amount of money to do right by a loved one.
>
> To be sure, many seniors caught up in the grandparent scam may be reluctant to discuss their situation, even if a teller tries to intervene. They're told by scammers to say nothing.
>
> How could [things] have gone differently? Well, what if the teller had discreetly raised the possibility of the grandparent scam?
>
> What if the teller had suggested that if Macaione had received such a call, he might want to phone his relative before transferring funds? What if he said the bank would be happy to provide a private office from which such a call could be made then and there?
>
> These few simple steps would have saved Macaione $27,000.

David Lazarus, "Banks Should Do More to Protect Seniors from 'Grandparent Scam,'" *Los Angeles Times*, January 14, 2020. www.latimes.com.

ensure that people trying to get access to an online account are who they say they are.

The arrest of 281 people in the reWired operation still makes only a minor dent in the online scam industry. The scams are simply too profitable to go away. And while they are increasingly

VIEWPOINT

Family Members Need to Help Protect the Elderly from Online Scams

Banks and other businesses can only do so much to protect people, and especially the elderly, from online scams. Family members need to step up to help parents, grandparents, or other elderly relatives avoid online scams and fraud. Carrie Kerskie, an expert on identity theft and internet safety, describes measures that families should take to prevent online scammers from taking advantage of older relatives.

> First, it's important to understand that your parents probably have a different perspective on fraud and scams than you do. . . . Unfortunately, it is this blind trust and false sense of security that makes seniors an easy target for scammers. . . .
>
> Ask Mom and Dad if they have ever searched their name on the internet. If not, do this quick experiment with them. This will help them see firsthand how much information is readily available about them online. . . .
>
> Talking with your parents (as opposed to talking at your parents) goes a long way. . . . By engaging them in conversation instead of telling them what to do, you are widening their perspective on their own terms. . . . If they do happen to receive a sketchy phone call or email one day, perhaps they will think twice about offering up any personal information.

Carrie Kerskie, "How to Talk to Your Parents About Fraud," *Aging Care*, October 11, 2019, www.agingcare.com.

professional looking, they do not require lots of technological know-how. "It's relatively easy to learn the techniques," notes technology writer Lily Hay Newman, "since the schemes are all intentionally low-tech and depend fundamentally on classic scams that prey on human biases and weaknesses."[40]

The Role of Banks in Foiling Online Scams

Cybersecurity experts stress that banks and lenders also have a large stake in stopping online scams that involve wire transfers. Often banks are blamed by frustrated customers who have fallen for fraudsters. This scenario played out in 2018, when Austin businessman Frank Krasovec lost $450,000 in an email scam conducted while he was in Asia on a business trip. Hackers broke into his company's computers and sent email messages to Krasovec's personal assistant, directing her to make wire transfers to an account in Hong Kong. PlainsCapital Bank in Austin, Texas, where Krasovec had opened a $1 million line of credit, called his assistant to double-check the transfer request before putting it through. Yet Krasovec sued anyway, claiming the bank should have done more to prevent the fraudulent transfer—such as calling him, not his assistant. In court filings, PlainsCapital declared that Krasovec must repay the money. The bank insists the loss was "undoubtedly the fault of [Krasovec's] own failure to implement appropriate internal controls to prevent his company and its employees from falling victim to a third-party scam."[41] According to the American Bankers Association, banks generally are not required to refund losses due to fraudulent wire transfers.

Banks remain eager, however, to educate their customers about online scams. For example, they emphasize that wire transfers, the preferred form of payment in many scams, are immediate and irreversible. Once funds are transferred, the bank cannot get them back, even if the transaction is a fraud. Banks urge customers to use multifactor authentication and to avoid sending money to people or companies whose information cannot be verified. They also warn about giving out account information or personal data in any circumstances.

High-Tech and Low-Tech Responses

A thriving industry has grown up around the effort to detect and prevent online scams. Companies are especially wary about phishing scams in all their varieties. Tech firms constantly update antivirus software to curtail malware before it can infiltrate a computer. Mailbox providers and individual users of business email employ so-called spam filters to weed out potentially dangerous spam emails that could include phishing links. Spam email, or junk email, consists of unsolicited messages that are sent in large numbers to addresses collected from websites, customer lists, hijacked address books, and other sources. "A big reason that it is so important for spam to be filtered is because it can contain malicious content that can spread viruses and cyber attacks," says Jarred Injaian of the email security firm SocketLabs. "One email can very easily take down a large corporation, so businesses need the best security they can get."[42] Today's spam filters check for trigger words or phrases often used by spammers, such as "dear friend," "risk free," and "special offer," as well as flagging header information that indicates the sender is suspect. Some can retrace an email's path to the recipient to see if it made any dubious stops along the way.

> "One email can very easily take down a large corporation, so businesses need the best [email] security they can get."[42]
>
> —Jarred Injaian, a writer for the email security firm SocketLabs

Companies are also banding together to share information about phishing schemes and other online scams. More than one thousand firms have joined the Anti-Phishing Working Group, an international organization that researches and shares data about cybercrime. The group consists of businesses that have been victimized by phishing attacks, companies that make cybersecurity products, law enforcement agencies, trade associations, and communications firms. Cybersecurity experts advise companies on how to avoid the most frequently used email and wire transfer scams.

Some tech firms are offering cutting-edge solutions to phishing attacks. A company called ZapFraud scans emails with so-called natural-language analytics. Rather than flag key words, its software searches for story lines used by scammers. Messages that refer to a large sum of money, a surprise need for funds, or a request for immediate action are targeted. "Those are the hallmark expressions of one particular fraud e-mail," says Markus Jakobsson, the founder of ZapFraud. "There's a tremendous number of [spam]

Many banks and other businesses rely on seminars to educate their employees about online scams and the importance of following security procedures.

e-mails, but a small number of story lines."[43] The company hopes one day to protect individual computer users with automated email filters that can detect malicious content in text messages, social media exchanges, and chats on dating sites.

For now, many businesses trust more low-tech methods to stave off phishing attacks and other online mischief. Stacey Coyne, vice president for cash management at Rockland Trust in Boston, Massachusetts, educates the bank's staff with seminars on fraud. She says many online schemes succeed because people get sloppy with regard to security procedures. "Too many people are too busy and they're using computers and email as their primary source of communication," says Coyne. "Unfortunately, that leaves them vulnerable in many situations when they could simply call someone on the phone to verify and substantiate any financial transaction."[44] She recommends practical steps, such as cleaning off one's desk at the end of each day to make sure sensitive papers do not fall into the wrong hands and checking company bank balances daily to flag any suspicious transfers or charges. Coyne also requires her employees to make sure that clients and vendors are following the same security protocols as they are. "You may be doing all you can to secure your financial information and protect your identities and so forth, but what are your vendors doing?" Coyne asks. "When you issue them a check, are they adhering to the same policies?"[45]

An Increasing Urgency to Stop Scammers

Stopping online scams is a huge priority for global law enforcement agencies, banks, businesses, and individuals. In the United States the FBI gathers reports on online scams via its IC3 website. The FBI partners with law enforcement from many different nations to disrupt scam networks with large-scale efforts like Operation reWired. Banks and private firms also emphasize high-tech and low-tech methods to foil scammers and email phishing schemes. As more business is conducted online, the urgency of protecting against online scammers is certain to increase.

CHAPTER FIVE

Avoiding Online Scams

Anyone can fall prey to email scammers, even well-known television personalities. In February 2020 Barbara Corcoran, a judge on the popular reality TV show *Shark Tank*, came close to losing nearly $400,000 in an online phishing scam. The scam was a targeted attack called spear phishing, which makes use of personal information. Corcoran's bookkeeper received a legitimate-looking email containing an invoice for a real estate payment. The scammer, pretending to be Corcoran's assistant, continued to exchange messages with the bookkeeper until the payment went through via wire transfer. When Corcoran learned of the transfer, she did not blame the bookkeeper. She pointed out it was the "result of a fake email chain sent to my company. It was an invoice supposedly sent by my assistant to my bookkeeper approving the payment for a real estate renovation. There was no reason to be suspicious as I invest in a lot of real estate."[46]

In this instance, the story had a happy ending. The German bank that Corcoran's bookkeeper used to wire the payment froze the transfer before it reached the scammer's Chinese bank account. Corcoran's bank, suspecting fraud, had asked for the transfer to be frozen so its staff could investigate. As a result, Corcoran escaped becoming an embarrassing statistic. According to the FBI's 2019 Internet Crime Report, more than 114,000 victims got caught in phishing scams, losing a total of almost $60 million. The high-profile incident also led to another positive outcome: it raised public awareness about how to avoid phishing attacks and other online scams.

Preventing a Phishing Attack

Falling for phishing schemes is all too common in today's business world. At least 3.4 billion fake emails are pumped out daily worldwide. And according to a survey by the business app company GetApp, almost half of all workers in American firms have clicked on fraudulent links attached to phishing emails. The phishing attack on Corcoran's business was typical in many ways. The scammer used social engineering, in the form of a fake email with a malicious link, to gain access to Corcoran's computers. That

Even well-known personalities, such as Barbara Corcoran (shown), a judge on the reality TV show Shark Tank, *can be targeted by online scammers.*

enabled the scammer to find out the names and email addresses of Corcoran's bookkeeper and assistant. The scammer then created a fake email address that was nearly identical to the address of Corcoran's assistant—except for one misplaced letter. The scam would have worked had Corcoran's bank not taken steps to double-check the large transaction. Cybersecurity experts say it often takes a team effort to foil online scammers.

A common mistake companies make is not training their personnel on how to spot phishing scams. Experts urge businesses to train their employees by presenting mock phishing scenarios so they understand how online scammers operate. Mike Meikle, a partner at the cybersecurity firm SecureHIM, says companies often do not take anti-phishing programs seriously enough. "A big compo-

The Limitations of 2FA

Two-factor authentication has long been considered the best defense against online phishing scammers. Yet a new phishing scam has managed to steal personal data from thousands of Citibank customers despite the company's use of 2FA. Cybersecurity experts say it shows the limits of even the best anti-phishing efforts when determined hackers are on the job.

In the Citibank scam, users who arrive at the phishing site are confronted by a Citibank log-in page that looks exactly like the real thing. The fake page asks for the user's log-in information and personal data as well as a one-time PIN to verify identity. This PIN serves as the second authentication. The sophisticated scammers are able to steal this number and enter it into the user's genuine Citibank account, thus gaining access. They then can steal money, change the account's address, or open other accounts under fake names. To foil this new phishing attack, users must know to check the URL of the log-in page against their bank's URL—a practice unfamiliar to most users.

Josephine Wolff, assistant professor at the Rochester Institute of Technology, says the new phishing scams should not cause people to lose all faith in 2FA. "The fact that two-factor authentication can be compromised through fairly straightforward, widely used tactics is no reason to stop using it," she says. "After all, no security tool is perfect. As long as it significantly decreases the likelihood of account compromises, two-factor authentication is still worth using."

Josephine Wolff, "Two-Factor Authentication Might Not Keep You Safe," *New York Times*, January 27, 2019. www.nytimes.com.

nent of protecting against phishing is employee training that actually works," says Meikle. Most such training is rather boring and often is not retained by employees, as Meikle explains. "If the training is given online the employees rapidly click through the content, ignoring most of the information. . . . If actually given in person, the training is usually a deck of PowerPoint slides in small font narrated by an uninterested speaker for an hour."[47]

> "A big component of protecting against phishing is employee training that actually works. If the training is given online the employees rapidly click through the content, ignoring most of the information."[47]
>
> —Mike Meikle, a partner at the cybersecurity firm SecureHIM

Above all, employees need to be wary of emails with links or attachments from people they do not know. They should remember that no legitimate employee, client, or website would ask for their password by email. Workers should also avoid careless internet browsing on company computers. A visit to one fraudulent website risks compromising the security system for the entire firm. Google helps defend business networks around the globe with its system of Safe Browsing Alerts. This service notifies a company's network administrator when it detects a suspicious URL that might include malware or social engineering links.

Technology and Two-Factor Authentication

Technology is vital to foiling phishing attacks. Spam filters that detect viruses in email, web filters that block malicious websites, and updated security patches for computer networks are all helpful tools for cybersecurity. New software products can even send corporate staff members fake phishing emails to test their ability to respond correctly. However, as Greg Scott of Infrasupport Corporation says, not even the best technology can eliminate the risk of phishing scams completely:

> In a company with, say, 1000 employees, that's 1000 possible attack vectors. The [information technology]

department can set up inbound spam filtering and outbound web filtering. They can run security drills, education campaigns, and spend enormous amounts of money to monitor traffic in detail. These are all helpful, but all it takes is one person, one time, to become careless and fall prey to an online con job—which should be the real name for a phishing attack. . . . So how to prevent them is the wrong question to ask. A better question is, how to limit the damage any successful phishing attack can cause.[48]

One of the best defenses against a phishing attack is two-factor authentication, or 2FA. This extra layer of security ensures that a person trying to access a network or online account has clearance to do so. In 2FA, as in other systems, users first enter their user name and a password. But then, instead of gaining ac-

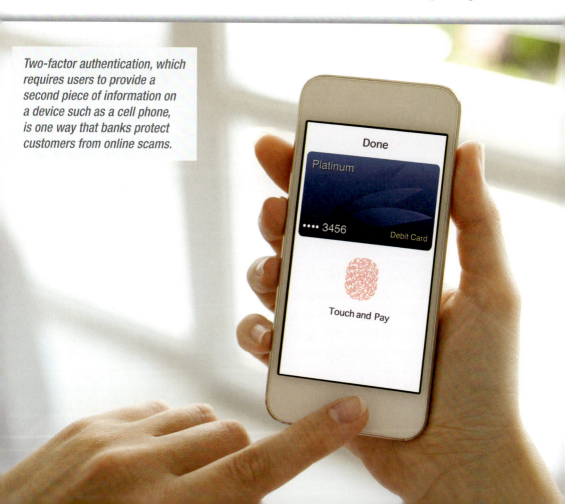

Two-factor authentication, which requires users to provide a second piece of information on a device such as a cell phone, is one way that banks protect customers from online scams.

cess at once, users must provide a second piece of information. This can be one of three types: something they know, such as a personal identification number (PIN), a password, or an answer to a secret question; something they have, such as a token, a credit card, or a smartphone; or something physical, such as a fingerprint, iris scan, or voice print. Banks and credit card companies use 2FA when users log in to their accounts. Often they email or text a code to the user that must be keyed in immediately to work. Despite experts' endorsement, many firms have yet to adopt 2FA. According to the GetApp research, only 64 percent of those surveyed said they currently use 2FA to protect their systems, leaving nearly one-third of users needlessly vulnerable. 2FA is not foolproof, but it does manage to foil most phishing attempts.

Foiling a Tech Support Scam

A phishing ploy that often catches individual users is the tech support scam. For young people especially, the sudden appearance of a pop-up window warning about a computer virus can be alarming. A person's natural reaction is to follow the directions on the screen to eliminate the threat quickly. But this is exactly what the scammers want—an emotional response that ends up giving them access to personal data.

The pop-ups crowd the computer screen and make it difficult to close the window. They may look like an error message from the computer's operating system or may include a logo associated with a trusted company, such as Microsoft, Apple, or an antivirus tech firm. Usually, they display a message explaining that the user's device has been infected with malware. For assistance in removing the malware, the user is given a toll-free phone number to call. The goal is to scam the user into paying a fee or subscription price to fix the problem. Users who call might also be told to pay with a gift card.

To foil a tech support scam, users should examine pop-up messages closely. Fraudulent messages often contain misspellings, bad grammar, or odd phrasings. Users also can conduct an online search for the phone number or business name on the pop-up to see if it is genuine. It is important that the user *not* call the displayed number. Legitimate pop-up messages from official antivirus products never require the user to call a toll-free number. Nor do antivirus companies make unsolicited calls about computer issues. And products that detect malware, like Norton and Bitdefender, are generally included in the subscription price. No further payment is necessary.

If a person has been scammed into paying for tech support, there are procedures to follow. The user should contact the bank or credit card company to cancel the transaction. If scammers have gained access to the user's computer, it is important to update the computer's security software immediately. Then a scan should be run to delete any malware. In case scammers have stolen a user name or password, these should be changed at once. Tech support scams should also be reported to the FTC, which uses such information to assemble cases against rings of online scammers around the world. Microsoft and other tech companies offer all the assistance they can for law enforcement efforts. "These tech support scams are truly a global problem, and Microsoft has been really committed to addressing them," says Courtney Gregoire, assistant general counsel for Microsoft's digital crimes unit, "because at the end of the day, they really do risk having consumers lose confidence in technology."[49]

> "These tech support scams are truly a global problem, and Microsoft has been really committed to addressing them, because at the end of the day, they really do risk having consumers lose confidence in technology."[49]
>
> —Courtney Gregoire, assistant general counsel for Microsoft's digital crimes unit

Protecting Against a Romance Scam

Millions of people today are relying on technology, by way of dating apps and social networking sites, to find romance. Through

To protect themselves, those involved in online dating should keep one or more close friends informed about the relationship.

hours and hours of online chatting, they develop strong emotional attachments to someone they have never met in person. And if they find out the budding romance is just a trick to get them to send money, their sense of betrayal and embarrassment can be overwhelming. People who have fallen for a romance scam are often reluctant to discuss it even with close friends or relatives.

Before signing up for online dating, people should be aware of the hazards. Americans lose more money in romance scams than in any other kind of online fraud. In 2019 the FBI received about 19,500 complaints about online dating scams, along with reported losses of $475 million. Experts note that romance scammers perform detailed research on a person's likes and dislikes to increase their appeal and sway their victims. Even normally cautious people can be deceived. "There were a couple of times when I said . . . are you scamming me?" June Miller recalls about a man she met online. "And he would say . . . 'baby how can you think that, you know I love you.'"[50] Miller eventually found out that everything about him, from his profile to his heartfelt declarations, was fake. But by then she had been swindled out of almost half a million dollars.

> "There were a couple of times when I said . . . are you scamming me? And he would say . . . 'baby how can you think that, you know I love you.'"[50]
>
> —June Miller, who lost almost half a million dollars in an online dating scam

To protect themselves, those involved in online dating should keep one or more close friends informed about the relationship. And friends' concerns should be taken seriously. Someone on the outside may be more likely to spot a fraud. At the beginning, users should do their own research about their online love interest. A profile picture can be checked by doing a reverse image search on Google. A photograph linked to another name or mismatched details is a sure sign of a scam. Snippets of the love interest's messages can also be checked online to see if they have appeared elsewhere. Likewise, people should look into any claims about employment. A bit of research can verify whether the person actually works where he or she claims to work. Boasts about wealth or world travel should be regarded skeptically.

Most important, those dating online should not allow themselves to be rushed into anything. Requests for money, in any form and for any reason, are a major red flag. Individuals should never transfer or wire money to an online love interest. If there are any signs of a romance scam, communication should be cut off at once. Victims should contact their bank if they

> "Be cautious if it's too good to be true and go into a relationship cautiously. Hopefully you find someone, but do so cautiously."[51]
>
> —Chad Hunt, FBI special agent, on the best approach to online dating

believe they have made payments to a scammer. Overall, online dating should be approached with great care. "Be cautious if it's too good to be true and go into a relationship cautiously," says FBI special agent Chad Hunt. "Hopefully you find someone, but do so cautiously."[51]

A Sober Look at Emotional Appeals

Animal lovers find it hard to resist charity ads featuring abandoned pets. Their hearts go out to animals that have been mistreated, and they are ready to help with checkbook in hand. Online scammers, knowing how compassion can overwhelm people's better judgment, design their appeals to take advantage of strong

Double-Checking GoFundMe Appeals

GoFundMe, an online crowdfunding platform, has helped many people escape financial ruin from accidents and illnesses. In 2018 one especially heartwarming tale went viral. A homeless veteran named Johnny S. Bobbitt Jr. spent his last few dollars to buy gas for a stranded young woman in Philadelphia. To repay him for his kindness, the woman, Katelyn McClure, decided to start a GoFundMe account for Bobbitt. Learning about the story online, more than fourteen thousand donors gave more than $400,000 to help Bobbitt turn his life around. However, it soon transpired that the story was a scam. The incident about running out of gas never happened, and a widely shared photo turned out to have been staged. McClure and her boyfriend—not Bobbitt—ended up blowing almost all the funds on trips, gambling, jewelry, and a luxury vehicle.

Although GoFundMe is legitimate, it can be exploited for moneymaking scams. The company suggests looking closely at each story before donating. Of particular importance is how the organizer is related to the recipient of the donations. Organizers who are sponsoring several GoFundMe campaigns at once may be suspect. It also helps to conduct a reverse image search on Google. Photos may be faked or taken from unrelated sources. According to Hillary K. Grigonis, who writes for the website Digital Trends, "GoFundMe isn't a bad platform—and in cases that involve criminal charges donors receive refunds—but . . . donors should be skeptical enough to do some digging before donating."

Hillary K. Grigonis, "How to Protect Yourself from GoFundMe Scams Before Donating," Digital Trends, April 10, 2019. www.digitaltrends.com.

emotions. The supposed recipients can be small children struck by poverty or illness, or they can be victims of recent disasters, including floods, hurricanes, and wildfires. Before donating to online charities, users should always do some digging for signs of a scam. Often scammers employ names that sound like genuine charities. Lists of legitimate charities covering various purposes can easily be found online. When examining a charity, donors should also look for details about how the money will be used.

One frequent trick used by online charity scammers involves emails congratulating people for donations they never made. This can make the recipients feel guilty and prompt them to make a first donation. Donations should never be made in cash, by gift card, or by wire transfer—the preferred methods of scammers. Also, donations should be made one at a time. Donors should ensure they are not signing up for recurring payments.

Today cyberspace is teeming with scams, and avoiding them requires a sharp eye and common sense. Phishing scams present perhaps the greatest danger, with the ability to commandeer computer networks and steal huge amounts of money and personal data. Users should exercise extreme caution when confronted with phishing emails or pop-up windows. Online dating, with its many opportunities for scammers, also must be approached warily. Everything from charity appeals to shopping sites online should be examined carefully before users part with their cash. A skeptical attitude can save people a great deal of money and embarrassment.

SOURCE NOTES

Introduction: A Scam on Online Gamers

1. Quoted in Cody Miller and Gabby Hart, "Authorities Warn Parents, Children of Scams Targeting 'Fortnite' Gamers," News3 Las Vegas, March 4, 2019. https://news3lv.com.
2. Quoted in Miriam Cross, "6 Scams That Prey on the Elderly," Kiplinger, November 26, 2019. www.kiplinger.com.
3. Quoted in Brian Barrett, "*Fortnite* Scams Are Even Worse than You Thought," *Wired*, October 29, 2018. www.wired.com.

Chapter One: The Growing Problem of Online Scams

4. Quoted in Ian Duncan and Colin Campbell, "Baltimore City Government Computer Network Hit by Ransomware Attack," *Baltimore (MD) Sun*, May 7, 2019. www.baltimoresun.com.
5. Quoted in Ian Duncan, "Baltimore Estimates Cost of Ransomware Attack at $18.2 Million as Government Begins to Restore Email Accounts," *Baltimore (MD) Sun*, May 29, 2019. www.baltimoresun.com.
6. Quoted in Shannon Houser, "Online Shopping Warning: 'It Pays to Be Very Careful When You Are Shopping Online,'" Cleveland 19 News, November 28, 2019. www.cleveland19.com.
7. Quoted in Kari Paul, "As Alleged $46M Online-Dating Scam Shows, Lonely-Hearts Are the Biggest Target for Scam Artists in America," MarketWatch, August 24, 2019. www.marketwatch.com.
8. Quoted in Paul, "As Alleged $46M Online-Dating Scam Shows, Lonely-Hearts Are the Biggest Target for Scam Artists in America."
9. Quoted in Lily Hay Newman, "Nigerian Email Scammers Are More Effective than Ever," *Wired*, May 3, 2018. www.wired.com.
10. Riya Sander, "Ten Types of Phishing Attacks and Phishing Scams," IT Pro Portal, November 25, 2019. www.itproportal.com.

11. Quoted in Megan Leonhardt, "'Nigerian Prince' Email Scams Still Rake In over $700,000 a Year—Here's How to Protect Yourself," CNBC, April 18, 2019. www.cnbc.com.

Chapter Two: How Victims Are Harmed by Online Scams

12. Quoted in Yuka Hayashi, "Scammers Find More Opportunities on Internet Marketplaces," *Wall Street Journal*, September 29, 2019. www.wsj.com.
13. Quoted in Carley Gordon, "Man Loses Life Savings to Scammer," Nashville News 4, August 5, 2019. www.wsmv.com.
14. Quoted in Gordon, "Man Loses Life Savings to Scammer."
15. Quoted in Caroline Balchunas, "Mount Pleasant Woman Warns Others After Losing Life Savings," ABC 4 News, October 10, 2019. www.abcnews4.com.
16. Quoted in Balchunas, "Mount Pleasant Woman Warns Others After Losing Life Savings."
17. Quoted in Jonah Kaplan, "Buying Pot Online? Risks Go Beyond Breaking the Law," ABC 11 News, August 9, 2019. www.abc11.com.
18. Quoted in US Food and Drug Administration, "FDA Takes Action Against 53 Websites Marketing Unapproved Opioids as Part of a Comprehensive Effort to Target Illegal Online Sales," June 5, 2018. www.fda.gov.
19. Quoted in Frank Abagnale, "Stolen Medical Records Lead to Patient Identity Theft," AARP, August 15, 2019. www.aarp.org.
20. Gail Buckner, "Scammers Want Your Medical Records . . . Here's Why," Fox Business, April 14, 2014. www.foxbusiness.com.
21. Quoted in Nina Culver, "Couple Lose Life Savings in Sophisticated Scam," *Spokane (WA) Spokesman-Review*, June 14, 2015. www.spokesman.com.
22. Quoted in Culver, "Couple Lose Life Savings in Sophisticated Scam."
23. Quoted in Jaime deBlanc-Knowles, "The Fraud Examiner: All Is Not Lost: Fraud Victims, Emotional Stress and the CFE,"

Association of Certified Fraud Examiners, July 2015. www.acfe.com.

Chapter Three: Why People Fall for Online Scams

24. Quoted in Katie Heaney, "What It's Like to Lose a Million Dollars to an Online Dating Scam," The Cut, April 11, 2019. www.thecut.com.
25. Amy Fontinelle, "Romance Scams Are Costing People More than Heartache," The Ascent, December 10, 2019. www.fool.com.
26. Fontinelle, "Romance Scams Are Costing People More than Heartache."
27. Quoted in Steven Melendez, "The Awful, Fast-Growing Tech Scams Fleecing the Elderly Out of Millions," *Fast Company*, May 10, 2019. www.fastcompany.com.
28. Quoted in Melendez, "The Awful, Fast-Growing Tech Scams Fleecing the Elderly Out of Millions."
29. AARP, "Tech Support Scams," March 11, 2020. www.aarp.org.
30. Frank T. McAndrew, "Why 'Nigerian Prince' Scams Continue to Dupe Us," The Conversation, August 3, 2018. www.theconversation.com.
31. McAndrew, "Why 'Nigerian Prince' Scams Continue to Dupe Us."
32. Stacey Wood, "Why So Many People Fall for Scams," BBC, July 27, 2018. www.bbc.com.

Chapter Four: Can Online Scams Be Stopped?

33. Quoted in Malvika Menon, "Bank Teller Who Foiled Love Scam Among 9 to Get Award," *Straits Times* (Singapore), November 26, 2019. www.straitstimes.com.
34. Quoted in Menon, "Bank Teller Who Foiled Love Scam Among 9 to Get Award."

35. Quoted in Kevin Kwang, "Singapore Police's New Anti-Scam Centre Wants to Hit Scammers Where It Hurts," Channel News Asia, August 30, 2019. www.channelnewsasia.
36. Quoted in FBI Archives, "Testimony: The FBI's Perspective on the Cybercrime Problem," June 12, 2001. https://archives.fbi.gov.
37. Quoted in Federal Bureau of Investigation, "2019 Internet Crime Report." https://pdf.ic3.gov.
38. Quoted in Maggie Miller, "Hundreds Arrested Worldwide in Operation Targeting Cyber Schemes," *The Hill* (Washington, DC), September 10, 2019. https://thehill.com.
39. Quoted in Federal Bureau of Investigation, "Worldwide Sweep Targets Business Email Compromise," September 10, 2019. www.fbi.gov.
40. Lily Hay Newman, "281 Alleged Email Scammers Arrested in Massive Global Sweep," *Wired*, September 18, 2019. www.wired.com.
41. Quoted in Rachel Louise Ensign, "Hackers Aid Rise in Wire-Transfer Scams," *Wall Street Journal*, February 24, 2020. www.wsj.com.
42. Jarred Injaian, "What Is a Spam Filter and How Does It Work?," SocketLabs, May 3, 2019. www.socketlabs.com.
43. Quoted in Maria Konnikova, "The Future of Fraud-Busting," *The Atlantic*, March 2016. www.theatlantic.com.
44. Quoted in Doug Bailey, "5 Low-Tech Ways to Protect Your Business from Cyber Fraud," *Boston Globe*, May 31, 2016. www.sponsored.bostonglobe.com.
45. Quoted in Bailey, "5 Low-Tech Ways to Protect Your Business from Cyber Fraud."

Chapter Five: Avoiding Online Scams

46. Quoted in Anthony Spadafora, "*Shark Tank* Host Falls Victim to Phishing Scam," TechRadar, February 28, 2020. www.techradar.com.
47. Quoted in Nate Lord, "Phishing Attack Prevention: How to Identify & Avoid Phishing Scams in 2019," *Data Insider* (blog), Digital Guardian, July 12, 2019. digitalguardian.com.

48. Quoted in Lord, "Phishing Attack Prevention."
49. Quoted in Melendez, "The Awful, Fast-Growing Tech Scams Fleecing the Elderly Out of Millions."
50. Quoted in Gina Silva and Kelli Johnson, "Dating App Dangers: FBI Warns Romance Scams Are on the Rise," Fox 10 Phoenix, February 13, 2020. www.fox10phoenix.com.
51. Quoted in Silva and Johnson, "Dating App Dangers."

ORGANIZATIONS AND WEBSITES

Anti-Phishing Working Group (APWG)—https://apwg.org

The APWG is a global coalition that works to eliminate cybercrime through data exchange, research, and public awareness. The group consists of more than twenty-two hundred institutions worldwide, including financial institutions, retailers, law enforcement agencies, trade groups, and online security providers.

Better Business Bureau (BBB)—www.bbb.org

The BBB is a nonprofit organization that helps consumers in the United States, Canada, and Mexico find businesses and charities they can trust. The BBB website offers advice on how to spot scams. The BBB Scam Tracker collects complaints about online scams and fraudulent businesses.

Federal Trade Commission (FTC)—www.ftc.gov

The FTC is a bipartisan federal agency with a dual mission to protect consumers and promote competition in the American economy. The FTC protects consumers by stopping unfair, deceptive, or fraudulent practices in the marketplace. The FTC's website contains the latest news stories about online scams and advice on how to avoid fraudulent schemes over the phone and on the internet.

Internet Crime Complaint Center (IC3)—www.ic3.gov

The FBI's IC3 provides the public with a reliable and convenient reporting mechanism to submit information about cybercrime and online scams. The FBI analyzes and distributes these reports to law enforcement and to the public. The IC3 website also contains an annual report on cybercrime and an archive of stories on internet scams going back to 2003.

National Consumers League—www.nclnet.org

The National Consumers League is a nonprofit group that promotes the interests of consumers and workers in the United States and abroad. Its website Fraud.org collects thousands of consumer complaints about online scams and other forms of fraud each month. Fraud.org shares these complaints with a network of more than two hundred law enforcement partners.

Stay Safe Online—https://staysafeonline.org

The Stay Safe Online website is part of the National Cyber Security Alliance, which seeks to educate and empower users at home, work, and school to use the internet safely and securely. The website features research about cybersecurity and tips on how to keep personal information safe from online scams.

FOR FURTHER RESEARCH

Books
Frank W. Abagnale, *Scam Me If You Can*. New York: Portfolio/Penguin, 2019.

Scot Augenbaum, *The Secret to Cybersecurity: A Simple Plan to Protect Your Family and Business from Cybercrime*. Nashville, TN: Forefront, 2019.

Adam Levin, *Swiped: How to Protect Yourself in a World Full of Scammers, Phishers, and Identity Thieves*. New York: Public Affairs, 2016.

Carole K. Zingula, *Surviving Online Dating Fraud: How I Recovered and the Lessons I Learned*. Phoenix: Peacock Proud, 2019.

Internet Sources
Amy Fontinelle, "Romance Scams Are Costing People More than Heartache," The Ascent, December 10, 2019. www.fool.com.

Lily Hay Newman, "Nigerian Email Scammers Are More Effective than Ever," *Wired*, May 3, 2018. www.wired.com.

Nathaniel Popper, "Ransomware Attacks Grow, Crippling Cities and Businesses," *New York Times*, February 9, 2020. www.nytimes.com.

Maxwell Strachan, "Millennials and Gen Z Get Scammed More than Their Grandparents, Sorry," *Vice*, January 3, 2020. www.vice.com.

Emma Witman, "The 11 Most Sophisticated Online Scams Right Now That the Average Person Falls For," Business Insider, March 25, 2019. www.businessinsider.com.

INDEX

Note: Boldface page numbers indicate illustrations.

AARP, 28, 39
Abagnale, Frank, 28–29
ages of victims, 8, 11–12, 40, 61
  See also elderly as victims
American Bankers Association, 52
Anti-Phishing Working Group
  basic information about, 53, 72
  monthly number of phishing attempts globally, 8
Anti-Scam Centre (Singapore), 45–46
antivirus software, 52
Ashley, Donald D., 27
Ausley Construction, 20

Baker, Steven, 17
Baltimore, Maryland, 10–11
banks as scam preventers
  education of customers, 52
  staff training, **54**, 54–55, 58–59
  stopping wire transfers, 44, 45, 56
  talking to victims before transferring funds, 44, 45–46, 50
  two-factor authentication, 58, **60**, 60–61
Baskin, Beverly, 26
Better Business Bureau (BBB)
  basic information about, 72
  income of victims and scams, 23
  number of shopping scam complaints received (2018), 13
  pet scam complaints, 14, 17
  Scam Tracker Risk Report, 14
  small business losses, 26
Bettke, James, 18
blackmail, 29
Bobbitt, Johnny S., Jr., 65
Boyer, Jennifer, 49
Bryant, Lisa, 22
Buckner, Gail, 29
Bureau of Justice Assistance, 46

business email compromise (BEC) schemes, 48–49
businesses
  email compromise schemes, 48–49
  losses to, from phishing scams (2019), 20
  small, as targets of phishing scams, 17–18, 26

cannabis products, 26–27
Capital One Financial Corporation, 8
Carter, David, 40–41
Center for Strategic and International Studies, 7
charity scams, 42, 65–66
Chow, Sheila, 44
Citibank, 58
clone phishing, 19
con (confidence) artists, 15
confidence tricks, 15–16
Corcoran, Barbara, 56–58, **57**
COVID-19 (coronavirus) protection scams, 31
Coyne, Stacey, 54–55
cybercrime, annual global cost of, 7

Democratic National Committee (DNC), 18
Dowden, Sandy, 17
drug mules, 36

education and romance scams, 34
elderly as victims, **30**
  of financial scams, 40–41
  of grandparent scams, 50
  losses to romance scams, 16
  medical information of, 28–29
  as percentage of scam victims, 11
  preventing successful scams on, 51
  reasons for being targeted, 8
  of tech support scams and, **37**, 37–39

eMarketer, 13
emotions of victims
   being targeted and, 36, 43
      compassion, 41–42, 65
      greed, 40–41
      loneliness, 33
      overconfidence, 34
      panic in tech scams, 37–39, **39**, 61
   impact on, 29–32, **30**, 63
   romance scams and, 16
Exposto, Maria Elvira Pinto, 36

FBI, **47**
   advice about internet safety and scams, 9
   businesses email scams, 17–18
   history of fighting internet crime, 46
   international operations and, 48–49
   losses to businesses from phishing scams, 20
   Operation reWired, 49, 50
   Operation Wire Wire, 49
   reporting cyber scams to, 9
   See also Internet Crime Complaint Center (IC3)
Federal Trade Commission (FTC)
   age of victims who lost money online, 11–12
   basic information about, 72
   employment claims of tech support scammers, 38
   losses to romance scams, 16, 34
   number of complaints about romance scams (2018), 16
   reporting tech scams to, 62
   residences claimed by scammers, 35
financial scams, 40–41
Fontinelle, Amy, 34, 35
foot-in-the-door technique, 42
Fortnite, 6–7, **7**
419 scams, 16–18, 41
Fraud Resource Center (AARP), 39

Gaffney, Francis, 31
GetApp, 57, 61
gift cards, scams involving, 23–25
GoFundMe appeals, 65
Goldstein, Sheryl, 10
Googe, Chip, 25
Google, 59
Gorham, Matt, 47
grandparent scams, 50
Gregoire, Courtney, 62
Grigonis, Hillary K., 65

hacking
   of Baltimore city government, 10–11
   of Capital One Financial Corporation data banks, 8
   phishing scams by, 18–20
   by Russians, 18
Hanna, Nick, 15
health dangers
   COVID-19 protection scams, 31
   medical records thefts, **28**, 28–29
   medications and supplements, 25–27
Herzberg, Ben, 9
Hunt, Chad, 65

IBM, 20
identity theft, from phishing scams, 11
income of victims, 23, **24**
Injaian, Jarred, 53
Internet Crime Complaint Center (IC3)
   amount Americans lost to online scams (2014–2018), 11
   amount Americans lost to online scams (2019), **12**, 47
   amount Americans lost to phishing scams (2019), 56
   amount Americans lost to romance scams (2019), 63
   basic information about, 9, 72
   creation of, 46

number of American victims of phishing scams (2019), 56
number of American victims of romance scams (2019), 63
number of complaints received (2017–2018), 11
number of complaints received (2019), 47
Recovery Asset Team, 47
romance scam warning by, 36
scammers posing as agents of, 47
website of, 46–47

Johnson, Debby Montgomery, 33, 34

Karpinsky, Gavin, 28–29
Karpinsky, Heather, 29
Kerskie, Carrie, 51
Krasovec, Frank, 52
Kubic, Thomas T., 46

Lazarus, David, 50
Lim Hao Jun, 45

Macaione, Sal, 50
malware
  clicking on links and, 47
  fear of, and tech support scams, 37–38
  phishing scams offering removal of, 61
  planted
    COVID-19 protection scams, 31
    fake security companies, 8
    Nigerian prince scams, 17
    phishing scams, 18, 19
    shopping scams, 14
    small businesses as targets of, 26
  in tech support scams, 38
marijuana, 26–27
McAfee, 7
McAndrew, Frank T., 41, 42
McClure, Katelyn, 65
McConnell, Sue, 13

medical records, thefts of, **28**, 28–29
Medicare, fraudulent billing of, 28–29
medications, 25
Meikle, Mike, 58–59
millennials as victims, 12
Miller, June, 64
money mules, 36
money wires. *See* wire transfers
Myers, Da'Quan, 27

National Consumers League, 73
National White Collar Crime Center, 46
natural-language analytics, 53–54
Newman, Lily Hay, 51
Nigerian prince scams, 16–18, 41

Ocala, Florida, 20
older adults as victims. *See* elderly as victims
online dating, 33, **35**, 63
  See also romance scams
online scams
  amounts lost to, 11, **12**
  characteristics of, 36–37
  forms of, 8
  types of, 8–9, **12**, 21
  See also specific types
online shopping, 13–14, **14**
Operation reWired, 49, 50
Operation Wire Wire, 49
opioid sales, 27

parcel scams, 44–45
Pedneault, Stephen, 31–32
pets, online sale of, 14, 17
pharmacies, bogus online, 25–26
phishing scams
  clone phishing, 19
  identity theft and, 11
  small businesses and, 17–18, 26
  spear phishing, 18–19, 20, 56–58
  typical, described, 18
  whale phishing, 19
Podesta, John, 18, **19**
pop-up ads, 61–62

prevention
    Anti-Phishing Working Group, 53, 72
    antivirus software, 52
    Google Safe Browsing Alerts, 59
    natural-language analytics, 53–54
    researching pop-up ads, 61–62
    romance scams, 63, 64–65
    spam filters, 52–53, 59
    Stay Safe Online, 73
    triggers in scam messages, 53–54, 61
    two-factor authentication, 58, **60**, 60–61
    web filters, 59
    See also banks as scam preventers
Puppy Find, 17

ransomware attack on Baltimore city government, 10–11
Recovery Asset Team (IC3), 47
romance scams, **35**
    age of victims, 16
    banks and stopping, 44, 45
    characteristics of, 15, 33, 34–35
    involving parcel scams, 45
    losses from, 16, 34
    money mules and, 36
    number of complaints to FTC about (2015–2018), 16
    prevention, 63, 64–65
    scammers' knowledge about victims, 34, 63–64
Russians, hacking by, 18

Safe Browsing Alerts (Google), 59
Sander, Riya, 19
Santucci, Larry, 8
Scam Tracker Risk Report (BBB), 14
Scott, Greg, 59–60
SEON, 7
Shadel, Doug, 38
shopping scams, 13–14, **14**, 22
Singapore, 44–46
Solum, Anja, 21
spam filters, 52–53, 59
spear phishing, 18–19, 20, 56–58

Statista, **12**
Stay Safe Online, 73

TechAdvisory.org, 40
tech scams, **37**, 37–39, 40, 61–62
teenagers as victims, 12, 40
trust and scams, 31, 37
Tucker, Laura, 6–7
two-factor authentication (2FA), 58, **60**, 60–61

United Kingdom, 34, 48
US Department of Justice. *See* FBI
US Food and Drug Administration (FDA)
    dangers of purchasing prescription medicines online, 27
    illegality of online opioid, 27
    operation of bogus online pharmacies, 25

V-Bucks, 6–7

Warren, Michael, 23
Wasser, Marv, 30–31
Wasser, Penny, 30–31
web filters, 59
Wenzler, Nathan, 16
whale phishing, 19
wire transfers
    banks stopping, 44, 45, 56
    money from, recovered by FBI, 49
    panic and, 37
    scams involving, 22, 30, 50, 52
    scams targeting businesses, 48, 49
Wolff, Josephine, 58
Wood, Stacey, 43
Wray, Christopher, 49

Young, Bernard C., 10
young adults as scam victims, 12, 40, 61

ZapFraud, 53–54
ZeroFOX, 6
Zobler, John, 20

PICTURE CREDITS

Cover: Alena A/Shutterstock.com

7: JJFarq/Shutterstock.com
12: Maury Aaseng
14: Casimiro PT/Shutterstock.com
19: Joseph Sohm/Shutterstock.com
24: Highwaystarz-Photography/iStock
28: sturti/iStock
30: Shutterstock.com
35: wavebreakmedia/Shutterstock.com
37: Rocketclips, Inc./Shutterstock.com
39: Shutterstock.com
47: Jer123/Shutterstock.com
48: AndreyPopop/iStock
54: TZIDO SUN/Shutterstock.com
57: JStone/Shutterstock.com
60: Denys Prykhodov/Shutterstock.com
63: Monkey Business Images/Shutterstock.com

ABOUT THE AUTHOR

John Allen is a writer who lives in Oklahoma City.